Praise for
Boundary Boss

"This powerful book is a clear path to deep healing work. If you're ready for true emotional freedom, let *Boundary Boss* show you the way. And thank you, Terri Cole! Your brilliant (and often hilarious!) guidance is a blessing to us all."

KRIS CARR
New York Times bestselling author

"This is a crash course in communication integrity—with so many clear and comforting techniques. Terri is a straight-talking psychotherapist who knows how to get us from unhealthy compromise to loving engagement."

DANIELLE LAPORTE
creator of *The Desire Map* and *How to Be Loving*

"Terri helps to make boundary setting tangible with practical steps to becoming a boundary boss. Her raw and relatable take on boundaries is a breath of fresh air. She presents clear guidelines on how to take boundaries to the next level."

MARIEL BUQUÈ, PhD
trauma psychologist

"With *Boundary Boss*, powerhouse healer and transformational therapist Terri Cole serves up the psychologically savvy medicine that you need to step out of destructive habits, stop people-pleasing, and set your soul free."

GABRIELLE BERNSTEIN
#1 *New York Times* bestselling author
of *The Universe Has Your Back*

"If you struggle with boundaries and are in need of a compass, seek no more! Terri Cole's exquisitely interesting, articulate, and profoundly practical *Boundary Boss* will rock your world. Her book masterfully engages the reader's heart and mind, while affirming and empowering their decisions to rise above their lifelong boundary-setting limitations."

ROSS ROSENBERG, M.ED., LCPC, CADC, CSAT
author of *The Human Magnet Syndrome*

"In a brilliant balance of stories, instruction, and opportunities to reflect, assess, and practice what we're learning, Terri Cole has written the book on boundaries we've all needed for-friggin'-ever. Somehow she also managed to deliver it in a super-loving, straight-to-the-point style that makes this deep and delicate topic easy to digest and apply. Five Stars."

ELIZABETH DIALTO
founder of the Institute for EMBODIED Living
and Wild Soul Movement

"Terri Cole's advice is game-changing! After having her on my *Off the Gram* podcast, I went home and broke up with a toxic friend, then wrote about it in my own book! Terri is the ultimate boundary boss and communication queen, and in this powerful book she shows us how to become the same. The world needs this book right now!"

MEAGHAN B. MURPHY
content chief for *Woman's Day* magazine
and author of *Your Fully Charged Life*

"Riddle me this: How can you possibly chase your dreams if you're bogged down by people-pleasing, codependent, and time-wasting tendencies of overworking and overfunctioning? Spoiler alert: You can't. If you're ready to create and live a life on YOUR terms, *Boundary Boss* is about to become your roadmap."

AMY PORTERFIELD
entrepreneur and host of
the *Online Marketing Made Easy* podcast

"Most people don't think about clear boundaries until they are violated. And then we feel stuck in our relationships. But imagine what your life would look like if someone had schooled you at an early age on the importance of boundaries and how to establish them? Terri Cole is that someone—and in *Boundary Boss*, she masterfully reveals how to find your most authentic voice, step into your power, and own your impact. You'll feel like you're being counseled by a dear, wise friend who truly has your back. This brilliant book is a must-read!"

DAVIDJI
author of *Sacred Powers*

BOUNDARY
BOSS

BOUNDARY BOSS

THE ESSENTIAL GUIDE
TO TALK TRUE, BE SEEN,
AND (FINALLY) LIVE FREE

TERRI COLE
MSW, LCSW

sounds true
BOULDER, COLORADO

Sounds True
Boulder, CO 80306

Sounds True is a trademark of Sounds True, Inc.

This book is not intended as a substitute for the medical recommendations of physicians, mental health professionals, or other health-care providers. Rather, it is intended to offer information to help the reader cooperate with physicians, mental health professionals, and health-care providers in a mutual quest for optimal well-being. We advise readers to carefully review and understand the ideas presented and to seek the advice of a qualified professional before attempting to use them.

Some names and identifying details have been changed to protect the privacy of individuals.

Published 2021, 2023

Book design by Maureen Forys, Happenstance Type-O-Rama
Illustrations © Wayne Fick, Wayne Fick Branding
Cover design by Wayne Fick and Rachael Murray
Author photo © Wendy Yalom

Printed in the United States of America

BK06619

ISBN: 978-1-64963-055-1

The Library of Congress has cataloged the hardcover edition as follows:

Names: Cole, Terri (Psychotherapist), author.
Title: Boundary boss : the essential guide to talk true, be seen, and
  (finally) live free / Terri Cole, Psychotherapist, LCSW.
Description: Boulder, CO : Sounds True, [2021] | Includes bibliographical
  references.
Identifiers: LCCN 2020037202 (print) | LCCN 2020037203 (ebook) | ISBN
  9781683647683 (hardcover) | ISBN 9781683647690 (ebook)
Subjects: LCSH: Assertiveness in women. | Women—Life skills guides. |
  Women—Psychology. | Self-actualization (Psychology) in women. | Stress
  (Psychology)
Classification: LCC BF575.A85 C65 2021 (print) | LCC BF575.A85 (ebook) |
  DDC 155.3/3392—dc23
LC record available at https://lccn.loc.gov/2020037202
LC ebook record available at https://lccn.loc.gov/2020037203

FSC
www.fsc.org
MIX
Paper | Supporting
responsible forestry
FSC® C103098

*First and foremost, this book is dedicated
to courageous women from around the
world who are committed to creating healthy
relationships and extraordinary lives. This book
is for you. I see you and am honored to guide you
on this transformational journey.*

*To my one and only, Victor Juhasz,
whose unwavering support, love, and culinary
skills made the writing of this book possible.*

*To my mother, Jan Cole,
who has always believed I could.*

If not you, who?
If not now, when?

CONTENTS

BOUNDARY BOSS BILL OF RIGHTS

- You have the right to say no (or yes) to others without feeling guilty.

- You have the right to make mistakes, to course correct, or change your mind.

- You have the right to negotiate for your preferences, desires, and needs.

- You have the right to express and honor all of your feelings, if you so choose.

- You have the right to voice your opinion even if others disagree.

- You have the right to be treated with respect, consideration, and care.

- You have the right to determine who has the privilege of being in your life.

- You have the right to communicate your boundaries, limits, and deal-breakers.

- You have the right to prioritize your self-care without feeling selfish.

- You have the right to talk true, be seen, and live free.

INTRODUCTION

DO YOU EVER SAY YES when you want to say no?

Do you prioritize other people's needs or desires above your own?

Do you often feel like you should be doing more in all areas of your life?

Are you overly invested in the decisions, feelings, and outcomes of the people you love?

Are you so resistant to asking for help that you end up doing most things yourself?

If any of these questions resonate, then you, my dear, are one of my over-functioning, over-giving, totally exhausted, sisters. You're also in exactly the right place.

Healthy, robust personal boundaries are the key to living a fulfilled, empowered, and self-directed life. Based on my personal and professional experience as a licensed clinical therapist for the last 23 years, I believe this is a fact. Every client who walks through my office doors, from the well-heeled millennial magazine editor, to the 40-something suburban mom, to the divorced CEO, has a different presenting problem: cheating spouse, overbearing boss, shitshow for family dynamics, and so on. Yet, at the heart of every single client's distress is the same problem: a lack of healthy boundaries. Fortunately, learning how to establish and enforce good boundaries is exactly what alleviates this pain. And it's totally doable.

Listen: if you are lacking in this all-important skill, you are not alone. I'm going to guess that you did not learn about healthy boundaries in school or at home, right? How can you possibly know what no one ever taught you?

Expecting to just *know* the language of healthy boundaries, without any instruction, is like thinking you could wake up fluent in Mandarin or Russian or any other language just by wishing hard enough. Not possible. Think of this book as a language intensive for effective boundaries, like Rosetta Stone®. With study and practice, you definitely can become fluent, and when you do, every part of your life will blossom. You will become more empowered in your relationships, especially the one you have with yourself. Which, as it turns out, is the most important relationship of all.

This book is a strategically designed how-to guide for becoming a full-fledged Boundary Boss (BB). A Boundary Boss is a woman who

- has a deep understanding of herself, including how her dysfunctional boundary patterns came to be and how they might be holding her back in the here and now;
- knows how to identify and transform any behavioral blocks standing between her and her true, heart-centered desires and their fulfillment;
- speaks truthfully, knowing that is the *only* way to create the life she wants and deserves;
- is committed to her own growth starting from exactly where she is right now.

(Note: This book was written with cisgendered women in mind, but I believe that anyone can benefit from the strategies and content. Boundary issues cross all gender expressions, in my experience.)

To align your behavior with your true desires, we're going to be spending some time clearing out what I refer to as your "basement"— in other words, your unconscious mind. Your basement stores beliefs and experiences that you've neatly tucked away and then promptly forgotten (at least consciously). Basement junk shapes your life in ways you're not entirely aware of. You can usually tell when it is in play because your reactions become supercharged or way out of proportion to the actual situation. Or you act against your best interests or better judgment. After the fact, you might think, *What the hell was that?* You may ignore your intuition and the signs from your body in an unconscious effort to avoid discomfort. This is called being human. If you're struggling with a present-day situation, I promise you that clearing the crap out of your basement will reveal relevant info and set you on a path to freedom.

It's normal to resist rehashing past experiences. Initially, many of my clients balk at my suggestion that we suit up and head to the basement, saying things like:

"It was so long ago; I should be over it."

"I don't want to blame my parents."

"I had a happy childhood!"

If I could teach you to become a successful Boundary Boss without the basement excavation, I *definitely* would. (And to be clear, our journey does not include blaming anyone.) Good news: I'll be guiding you the entire time, holding your hand, shining my headlamp to light our way. You got this, and I got you.

To set you up for success, let's spend some time understanding what this Boundary Boss journey entails—and why it matters.

Establishing, communicating, and maintaining healthy, vibrant, and flexible boundaries make it possible to have a deeply satisfying life. Without great boundaries, it's *impossible*. Yes, impossible. I am certain of this.

For those of you perpetually operating on get-it-done autopilot or afflicted by the disease-to-please, a phrase coined by renowned psychologist and women's issues expert Dr. Harriet Braiker, this may land as bad news. Yes, you will have to slow down and step out of the well-worn grooves of your comfort zone to know, express, and protect your authentic self. (Raise your hand if you're thinking, *Authentic self? What the hell is that?*) But as you become more confident in setting limits and speaking truthfully, you'll gain a deeper knowledge of and appreciation for your authentic self (she is a total rock star, btw). And what seemed like bad news will look like opportunity.

Often, unhealthy boundary patterns are rooted in a confusion about what's actually *your* responsibility. For example, we may think that someone else's distress or conflict is ours to fix, when, in fact, their emotional experience and problems are definitely *theirs* to deal with. That's *their* side of the street. This book is all about you and *your* side of the street.

When you're clear about what's yours to handle, the process of transformation becomes much more accessible. Your focused intention is the requirement for making these techniques work for you. For things to change, you have to be willing to try something new. This process requires effort, and you are worth it. I am mesmerized by your ability to create a life that thrills and fulfills the real you. I have no doubt, based on the success I've had with countless students and clients, that it's possible for you, too.

Here's How This Is Going To Work

In the first part of the book, we are gathering information and taking an honest inventory of all areas of your life, revealing the specific life experiences, influences, and misinformation that may be contributing to your boundary struggles. We will be unearthing your **Boundary Blueprint**, to illuminate the conscious and unconscious ways you currently relate to boundaries. These ways of relating are influenced by what you learned growing up, including how you were raised, what you observed in your family of origin, and the societal norms of your greater culture. Many people find this process truly liberating. This learned behavior is not your fault, but figuring it out now is definitely your responsibility. With the right tools and guidance, you will have the power to rewrite your blueprint.

In the second part, we move into becoming fluent in the language of boundaries and taking small steps informed by your new awareness. All of the tools, strategies, and scripts can be customized to suit your style and comfort level. There is no one-size-fits-all boundary strategy. You are unique, and so is the right way for you to relate to and express your boundary preferences and deal-breakers.

We also cover the step-by-step process for developing your **Proactive Boundary Plans**, those necessary strategies for shifting from reactive to proactive boundary behavior. We'll talk about how to handle people who attempt to trample on your boundaries long after you've clearly expressed your limits, and we'll discuss the instances in which the rules don't apply, specifically when interacting with people who are **Boundary Destroyers**, or narcissists and other difficult personalities. Every step of the way, I'll be right there with you, as your compassionate, loving (and kick-ass) guide.

As part of this process, you will be getting in touch with your inner child, the part of you that did not get her needs met in childhood. When I first heard about the concept of the "inner child," before I became a therapist, I wanted to dismiss it as BS. It sounded too precious and flimsy, like magical thinking. In truth, though, unresolved childhood injuries negatively impact our current relationships. Over time, I saw that the inner child needs tending in a very real way (more on this in chapter 8). All you need to do right now is be open to the idea that your responses to current things in your life might be driven by, say, five-year-old you. Would you let a five-year-old make major decisions for your marriage or family? Would you let a five-year-old decide your career moves? I don't think so.

This is where we need to have compassion for ourselves. Then, and only then, can we create the expansion necessary to become conscious of dysfunctional behaviors. Poking in the cobwebbed corners of the basement to discover potentially uncomfortable past memories is part of the process, but rest assured that the point is not to dwell in the past. If you connect the dots back far enough, you will find an incident or experience that needs your attention. Identifying original injuries leads you to acknowledge, process, and honor the inner child's experience. Understanding your early experiences can impact your present-day life in profoundly positive ways.

To remember to treat yourself with compassion, I give you a strategy (in chapter 6) to help you to *recognize* when the little kid in you might be activated so you can *release* the old reaction and choose a *response* from the grown-up you that is in your highest good. It's called the **3Rs (Recognize-Release-Respond)**.

If you are like any of the thousands of clients and students who have come before you, the revealing nature of this work will inspire a range of emotions—hope, exhaustion, anxiety, and excitement. You may feel selfish at times, especially when it comes to changing the unspoken agreements in your relationships and prioritizing your own feelings. For some, the idea of rocking the boundary boat kicks up feelings of fear, guilt, and shame. *Will I be ridiculed by the people I love? Am I rejecting them by unilaterally changing the rules of engagement?*

As you build this skill set, know that real, sustainable change happens step by step, not overnight. You will learn to make changes and shift behavior by simply taking the next right action, and then the next. There is quite a learning curve from part 1 (information gathering) to part 2 (transforming that info into new behavioral patterns and choices). So, patience and self-compassion are good companions as you go through the process of freeing yourself from deeply embedded, self-sabotaging attitudes and behaviors.

When you reflect on your boundary missteps, you may feel embarrassed, regretful, or ashamed. Please understand that your past behavior is not a reflection of who you are—just what you knew at the time. And this entire book and your personal transformation process are a no-judgment zone. If there are moments when you feel like a mess, I say, celebrate. You're doing something that 80 percent of the population will never do. Plus, you're human, pal. Cut yourself some slack.

Here's the thing, though: you're in charge of writing the instruction manual on you. That manual gets "read" by everyone you encounter. If you feel disrespected, undervalued, or taken for granted, that simply means it's time to rewrite your instruction manual, setting the bar higher for yourself and everyone else in the process. You can totally do it.

To set you up for success, I encourage you to create a safe and cozy space in your home where you can attend to your internal space. I call this sacred space the Zen Den. Your Zen Den is the perfect spot to meditate, journal, and do the integration exercises, which you'll learn more about below.

A Few Pointers on How to Use This Book

Whatever your reading style, let me be straight with you: this book is meant to be consumed in chronological order. Why? Because each chapter builds on the one before it.

To help you apply what you're learning, I offer tips, self-assessments, and exercises throughout each chapter. These are the same things I use with my clients and students, and they are essential to achieving your desired results.

True Talk Tips: Throughout each chapter, I recap the key concepts to keep you on track.

Back to You: Quick, on-the-fly self-assessments help you personalize information and apply it immediately to your unique experiences.

Boundary Boss in Action: At the end of each chapter, I offer two main ways to put your new knowledge into action. *Top of Mind* suggests ways to help you expand your self-awareness. *Go Deeper* offers integration exercises (continued at the back of the book) that help you create sustainable change (don't skip these!). Once in a while I also suggest something to help you *Get Inspired*, too.

Boundary Boss Bonus Bundle online: Go online to get exclusive mindfulness tools, guided meditations, and supplemental strategies at BoundaryBossBook.com/bonus.

My advice? Go at your own pace, take what works, and leave the rest. When things start to get hot, slow down, cool down, and breathe. Remember the tools you're learning and use them. Give yourself space and time, then come back when you're ready. Doing internal work can kick up intense feelings. Pay attention and listen. Ask yourself: Do I need to

- take a break?
- take a walk?
- call a pal or a professional?

Your mental health and emotional safety are your responsibility and must always be your highest priority. So, throughout our journey, *please take care of you.* My promise is that if you do the work, you will see and feel the positive results in your life and relationships.

Although mastering boundaries can take time, learning how to set and enforce them does not. If you stay the course, by the end of the book you'll have the skills and savvy to do just that. You will have systematically weeded out corrupted information that's been affecting your boundary behaviors. You will have transformed your limiting, habitual thought patterns into empowered, mindful beliefs and actions. You will have paved the way to positive, sustained changes that will bring more satisfaction, confidence, and peace to all of your relationships. And they'll be based on what you really want instead of some crap you've inherited. The self-knowledge you'll gain will powerfully influence the rest of your life.

Consider this book a love offering from my heart to yours. For over twenty years, I have witnessed this process transform lives, making the language and implementation of healthy boundaries accessible and effective. I see tangible results every single day, in my own life and in the lives of my clients. To date, I have guided thousands of women from all over to the globe to become their own Boundary Boss, their way. It's my life mission to guide you to living the one-of-a-kind, empowered life that only you can live.

Ready to dive in?

Let's go!

PART 1

Connecting

the Dots

to the Past

CHAPTER 1

From Boundary Disaster to Boundary Master

I WAS A BRIDESMAID EIGHT times in my twenties. *Eight.*

I should have politely declined at least half of those ugly-dress experiences, but I did not know how to say no. Or, "Hell, no," or even, "I'd love to celebrate your true love and all, but I have an urgent situation to handle." (Like, say, scraping the bottom of my change jar for subway fare since I was a broke 22-year-old trying to make it in New York City.) How could I afford to be in a wedding party with some gals I knew from waitressing back in the day? In truth, my fears of disappointing the brides-to-be were far greater than the reality of my paltry bank account balance. I didn't want to be seen as rude, insensitive, or, worst of all, not "nice." If I said no, I'd be rejecting the privilege of being chosen. Who was I to do *that*?

That fear alone spurred me to shell out thousands of dollars I didn't have (hello, credit card debt) to participate in rituals for people who wouldn't have even made the guest list for my housewarming party (if I'd had a house, that is). Not surprisingly, I felt burdened and resentful. These secretly held emotions would crop up at bachelorette parties, rehearsal dinners, or anytime I caught a glimpse of the teal green, poofy-shouldered '80s dresses hanging in the back of my closet, all of which I definitely would *not* wear again. For what?

The "honor" of not being able to speak my truth. Looking back, all I can say is, "F that, people."

My perpetual bridesmaid status was symptomatic of a larger problem that millions of women deal with: unhealthy boundaries. Yes, having difficulty establishing, enforcing, and communicating healthy limits in all areas of life is practically an epidemic. The cost of bad boundaries is immense. It leads to conflict-ridden, imbalanced relationships, a lack of agency over our own time, and general malaise. You got time for that drama, mama? No, you do not.

In the case of my disordered boundaries (and probably yours, too), my fear of disappointing others got in the way of basic common sense. I *could* have chosen differently. I *could* have set parameters around how I would spend my precious time and money. I *could* have said, "No, thank you. That dress is gross, and so is your fiancé." (He hit on me at the engagement party!) Let's just say, I had many options at my disposal, but there was one massive obstacle to flexing my boundary muscles: I didn't even know I had a choice.

Wherever you might be in your life, you have choices, too.

For the last two decades, I have practiced as a licensed clinical therapist, treating predominantly female clients suffering an array of boundary issues. From erratic, to too flexible, to not flexible enough, their boundaries are *disordered* in some way. Some clients are so independent and self-sufficient that they never ask for or allow others to help them do anything. They will stop cab drivers from lifting their heavy suitcase into the trunk or grocery-store baggers from bagging their groceries (things that are, literally, *their job*). "I got it, thanks," they'll say. Others suffer from a compulsive need to please the people in their life at the expense of their own well-being. Or overextending themselves to stay in the good graces of everyone (even people they barely like). This can materialize as saying yes when they want to say no, like agreeing to run the PTO fundraiser (again) even though they are simultaneously slammed at work and trying to sell their house.

BACK TO YOU:
How Do You Relate to Boundaries?

Below are some common boundary issues. See yourself in any?

- Do you ever say yes to requests, even though your gut is saying, "No, thanks"? "Yes, I'll show up for you (*while completely abandoning myself*). Sounds great, can't wait!"

- Do you inconvenience yourself for other people? "Sure, I'll watch your cat for a week because you don't want to pay a professional!" (*Even though staying in Brooklyn adds an hour to my commute, and your cat hates me. Okay, maybe it's mutual.*)

- If you have an issue with a pal's behavior, do you sidestep a tough conversation by casually avoiding them? "Oh, I'd love to see you, but work is so busy!" (*Even though my schedule is wide open for my drama-free pals.*)

- Do you engage in passive-aggressive expressions of anger instead of calmly expressing your feelings? "Whatever works for you. I changed my plans based on what you said originally, but it's totally fine!" ☺

- Are you so self-sufficient that you do everything for yourself, by yourself? "I got this!" (*Even though I am exhausted, bitter, and currently running through a mental list of who should help me based on my past generosity.*)

If you recognize yourself in any of these examples of unhealthy boundaries, rest assured you are not alone. Right now, we are gathering information about the unique way you relate to boundaries. This will illuminate where to focus your efforts.

Or they'll invite their alcoholic cousin to their birthday party even though they know it will end badly. From my professional background and personal history, I really get how *no* seems like such a simple word to say. Yet for so many, it can also be the hardest.

No matter how many memes we see in our social media feeds, such as, "*No* is a complete sentence!" or "You got this, gurrrrrl!" the reality of knowing and expressing our true selves is much more complex when bad boundaries have been our historical norm.

Bad boundaries are exhausting. They create dramas that suck our time and energy. As you likely already know, it takes a lot of effort to keep putting out fires in our personal lives. When we're caught up in our bad boundaries, though, we often don't realize that we're the ones who are inadvertently lighting these fires. To stop these distracting disruptions, we have to go back to our earliest influences—the scene of the crime, so to speak—where the original injuries and learning occurred.

To illustrate this concept of how original injuries lead to unhealthy boundaries and self-created conflicts, let's take a walk down memory lane. I will share a snapshot of how I moved from being a Boundary Disaster to a Boundary Semi-Disaster and finally to a full-fledged Boundary Boss. My hope is that you will recognize glimpses of your own life in my story and feel confident that you can also make the journey into Boundary Boss-dom, your way.

Watch and Learn

In my young life, I learned everything about disordered boundaries and ineffective communication from two people who had almost no life experience before they started raising kids. My mother was nineteen years old and three months into her freshman year of college when she became pregnant with my eldest sister. She dropped out of school permanently and married my father in the back office of a Presbyterian church in Glens Falls, New York. They proceeded to have three more daughters in less than six years. I'm the youngest.

Raising us in the New Jersey suburbs, my parents modeled traditional roles. My father was the provider, a white-collar upper-management type, who golfed on the weekends, drank too much (think: *Mad Men*–level martini consumption), and expected dinner on the table when he got home from work. My mother was a loving, compassionate, and protective stay-at-home mom, who raised us and all of our friends. My father made the money, and my mother handled everything else, including running the household and taking responsibility for our well-being.

Our family, like many families, was a perfect storm of covert communication and emotional dysfunction. My parents both came from families that avoided open discussions about anything painful or problematic. And there's the heart of the matter: ineffective communication skills lead to weak or disordered boundary skills.

Though my father wasn't violent or abusive, we all feared his disapproval. My mother was careful not to upset him. My sisters and I rarely heard his deep, rumbling voice unless there was a problem. All together I probably exchanged fewer than a hundred words with him before my parents got divorced when I was thirteen.

In general, his lack of communication translated to emotional unavailability. So even when he was there, he wasn't there to be with us. "Hey, sports fans!" was code for *I'm taking over the TV to watch golf now*. My sisters and I could have been engrossed in the last five minutes of *Grease* (picture it: right before Olivia Newton-John transforms from good girl to a butt-smoking, spandex-wearing vixen), but when we heard his "sports fans" cue, we knew there was only one acceptable response. "No problem. Byeeeeee!" None of us actually *liked* the fact that we couldn't watch the end of our movie, yet we acted like we didn't mind one bit. Speaking truthfully was not an option.

Often, the most powerful rules in families are the ones that are not explicitly stated. For example, in my family, it was crystal clear that my parents had an unspoken agreement about how each would operate: Dad was the breadwinner, and Mom was the nurturer and family manager. Perhaps the most significant silent pact in our household, though, was to avoid expressing anger directly. Just as I could sense that my ever-chipper mom was fearful of rocking the boat with my dad, I instinctively knew that anger was taboo.

Humans, even little humans, are wired to minimize exposure to perceived danger. My childhood training taught me to automatically read people and scan situations to assess the threat level to avoid conflict. *Anyone's* anger could be threatening. I actively avoided upsetting my father. Like my sisters, I didn't express my genuine feelings either. But emotions don't just—poof!—disappear because they're inconvenient or unacceptable in our family systems. They go underground. And that's not good.

In our household, four teenage girls acted out their repressed anger with door slamming, shit talking, and if my parents were out, an occasional fistfight. My older sisters also vented their anger (and the veiled feelings of the entire family system) dramatically, if indirectly, by running away, having bad boyfriends, doing drugs, and drinking. In these situations, witnessing my father's disapproval and my mother's anguish made a strong impression on me. I vowed never to be the cause of either. Not that I didn't do most of those things. I did. I just made sure that I never got caught.

Consequently, I learned to bury my true feelings. Adaptively, I transmuted them into more allowable ones (anger became sadness, for example) and ignored my gut instincts. This strategy kept me safe from disapproval and eased my primal fear of being kicked out of the clan if I dared to upend the unspoken rules. By the time I left for college, my unhealthy communication style, disordered boundaries, and questionable coping techniques were all I knew. I was a full-fledged Boundary Disaster.

BACK TO YOU:
What Were Your Forbidden Feelings?

Check the boxes next to any emotions that were discouraged, punished, or forbidden in your childhood.

◻ Happiness: joy, satisfaction, a sense of well-being

◻ Sadness: disappointment, hopelessness, disinterest

◻ Fear: unsafe, threatened, activated fight-flight-freeze response

◻ Disgust: revulsion, disapproval, rejection

◻ Anger: hostility, agitation, frustration

To become a successful Boundary Boss, you must allow yourself to feel *all* of your feelings. This starts with becoming aware of the ones that you'd rather not experience.

On My Own

In adulthood, my unhealthy boundary patterns continued. I became a master of indirect communication, using sarcasm, eye-rolling, and the occasional hostile lie, such as, "I said, I'm *fine!*" (Sound familiar?) I also became skilled at covert manipulation; meaning, those I was manipulating (usually my boyfriends) never realized I had my own secret agenda operating behind my it's-all-good facade. Covert manipulation ensured that I would get approval, avoid confrontation, and keep them happy. Meanwhile, I did whatever I wanted behind the scenes, such as spending time with old flames or clubbing in the city with my sisters (and "forgetting" to mention either). Attempting to control others and situations was a bid to feel safe. This strategy worked until it didn't. It's no coincidence that, after struggling with authentic expression throughout my childhood, I found my way to a therapist's couch in college and have stayed for the past thirty years.

TRUE TALK *Ineffective communication skills lead to weak or disordered boundary skills.*

I hadn't heard of the term *boundaries* when I entered therapy. Little did I know that my disordered relationship with limit-setting was affecting every area of my life, including how I socialized and how I communicated. Since college is a time when even non-alcoholics drink alcoholically, by my senior year, I had done my share of booze-induced puking, passing out, and blacking out. My father had set an example with his excessive drinking, which my fun-loving, out-of-control older sisters had followed. Starting at age fourteen, I was doing shots right along with them. By the time I got to college, I thought my booze-induced behavior was normal. My therapist, Bev, however, did not.

After weeks of my casually mentioning my alcohol-fueled exploits, Bev dropped a bomb on me. "If you do not seek help with a twelve-step program for your drinking, I will have to terminate our relationship," she said. *Wait, what?* Was my therapist breaking up with me?

As shocked as I was by her ultimatum, I was even more surprised at my visceral reaction to the thought of getting help: a full-body exhale. I was relieved. *So* relieved. Deep down, I knew the truth in my body long before my mind would even consider putting down my Miller Lite for good (don't judge! I was in college). Booze was hindering my growth and my happiness. My self-sabotaging behavior would continue as long as I attempted to drink away feelings of anger, sadness, and fear. With three months left of my senior year, I quit drinking.

Wide Awake

Being sober opened my eyes to the concept of healthy internal boundaries. Internal boundaries refer to how well or how poorly you regulate your relationship with yourself (more on them in chapter 7). For example, do you listen to your own needs first? Are you responsible for your behavior? For the first time in my life, I actually examined how I related to myself. I didn't even know having a relationship with one's self was a *thing*.

I also didn't realize that to create healthy boundaries in any other relationship, I needed to be a master of my internal boundaries and my relationship with myself. Now that alcohol wasn't clouding my perspective, I started to ask myself some difficult questions, such as:

- Do I keep my word and follow through on the commitments I make to myself? (Not really.)

- Do I keep my word to others in my life and do what I say I will do? (Not always.)

- How is my self-discipline, time management, impulse control, and emotional self-regulation? (Needs work.)

I was 22 years old with a ton of work ahead of me, but I was clear-eyed for the first time in my life. Therapy had inspired the most profound epiphany to date: no matter what cards I'd been dealt in this life, I could not only request a new hand, I could create an entirely new game.

That realization fueled my imagination and my transformation.

Passionate about self-exploration and personal improvement, I continued to see my first therapist, Bev, for years after graduation.

Every Monday night, like clockwork, I caught the 7 p.m. commuter train out of Penn Station in New York to her small town in Long Island, getting back to my apartment around midnight. That weekly effort directly reflected my belief that if I stayed on the self-discovery, self-healing course, my life would continue to get better. Yes! I could *choose* to live my life in a more empowered way. Still, I had miles to go in grasping exactly what that meant on a daily basis.

Smoke and Mirrors

At 25, my first real career job was in the bright, shiny, and blurred-boundary world of entertainment, working as a talent agent. Um, not exactly a hotbed of mental health. The clear-cut rules of engagement of the regular business world did not exist there. Socializing and partying after hours with casting directors and clients was part of the job description, blurring the lines between personal and professional. Despite my sobriety and therapy, I was still a Boundary Semi-Disaster.

Nevertheless, I kept on asserting my wobbly limit-setting skills. "No, you can't call me at three o'clock in the morning because someone forgot to put sparkling water in your dressing room." What I was only starting to comprehend was that, in fact, I had choices about how I let people treat me, both at work and in my personal life.

My in-process boundary skills didn't prevent me from fulfilling my ambitions, though. Steadily, I rose through the ranks, and five years later ended up running the New York operation for a bicoastal talent agency, negotiating five- and six-figure contracts for supermodels and celebrities. Amazing, right? Well, not exactly.

The reality behind my fancy title was painful. I had become a stressed-out workaholic, who often ate froyo for dinner and lit up one of my trusty Parliament 100s every time drama would erupt (pretty much all day long). In addition to managing the professional lives of clients, I often got involved in their personal dramas. I also felt responsible for fixing the lives of subordinates, close friends, and family. Unconsciously, I believed that the responsibility for their shit belonged on my already overburdened shoulders. I unofficially therapized everyone, including my romantically challenged mail carrier. Meanwhile, I was a hot mess, albeit an over-functioning one.

My breaking point came when I could no longer deny that I cared waaaay more about getting models into rehab, therapy, and eating-disorder clinics than I did about getting them a lucrative Pantene deal or a movie contract. I had evolved to valuing people over profit. I needed a drastic career change.

Wanting to build a career aligned with my burgeoning authentic self, I enrolled in New York University's Master of Social Work program. I couldn't afford to quit my day job, though. While in school full time, I was still running the television department for the Elite Modeling agency remotely and teaching acting as an adjunct professor at NYU's Tisch School of the Arts. Juggling grad school and two legit jobs simultaneously required me to assert my still-developing boundary skills daily, if not hourly.

To succeed as a teacher, I had to be crystal clear about my class rules (express boundaries/limits/expectations) and enforce them (no people-pleasing allowed). Being in grad school required further development of the internal boundaries that getting sober first revealed (keeping my word to myself). This meant being dialed in to and prioritizing my needs, preferences, and desires, and doing what I needed to do to succeed (sticking to my schedule, saying no to invitations, not dropping everything for every friend or family member in crisis).

Better boundaries also meant I had to delegate at the agency. This last bit was especially hard for a newly recovering control freak.

TRUE TALK *In changing your boundary behavior, you learn to recognize that you have a fuller range of choices at your disposal than you have realized or exercised until now.*

By the time I graduated two years later, though, I felt accomplished on many levels, especially with my newfound boundary acumen. I was 33 and very proud that I had come so far with limit-setting and interpersonal communication, but had no idea that life was about to serve up my biggest boundary test yet.

Plot Twist

Just as I was embarking on my new life chapter, the universe threw me a one-two punch that made me reexamine everything: the sudden death of my father and, shortly thereafter, a cancer diagnosis that sent me into two major surgeries and radiation therapy. All within a year.

The double whammy of losing my father and facing my own mortality in my early thirties sparked a major reckoning.

Despite my years of therapy, I still struggled with active codependency, a deeply ingrained habit of taking on others' problems as if they were my own, which was definitely a result of lingering disordered boundaries. Sure, I had learned to say "no, thanks" to certain invitations (ahem, reluctant bridesmaid no more), but I hadn't fully examined the internal experience of what happened when I put others' needs consistently above my own.

The years I'd spent orienting my life around other people had finally caught up with me. The chronic stress contributed to a potentially life-threatening health diagnosis. I needed space to exhale. To get that space, I had to go deep into how I had come to feel responsible for everyone and everything. I remember thinking to myself while waiting to get the diagnosis from my doctor, *There is so much more for me to learn and do. I so hope I don't run out of time.*

That's when the lights in the metaphorical room came on. Yes, I theoretically understood that I had *choices* about how to show up for others and myself, but I needed to exercise those choices more consciously than I had been. I had to. This epiphany was the final push I needed to get to boundary mastery. I now consider this period, from changing careers to my remission from cancer, as my own Boundary Bootcamp. I went through all the stages of boundary development—new self-awareness, followed by self-knowledge, self-acceptance, and self-compassion—to ultimately become a Boundary Master in less than a decade. My personal Boundary Boss journey has fueled my deep desire to lessen the suffering of others, to highlight where you absolutely have choices, and to show you how to make those choices with ease and grace. From my own experience, I know just how delicate, long, and sometimes winding the road to emotional wellness can be. Each turn along the way leads to increased self-understanding, which builds better boundaries. That's why I am passionate about teaching this uniquely transformative language. The blood, sweat, tears—and years—it took me to free myself drives my desire to give you the most direct and efficient route to boundary fluency. In the words of writer Richard Bach, "You teach best what you most need to learn."

Most women, like my younger self, don't even realize the root of their unhappiness, let alone know how to create change. Consciousness is always the first step. We can't heal what we're not aware of, after all. That's why we're here.

> **TRUE TALK** *No matter what your boundary patterns are currently, it is possible for you to learn how to establish healthy, vibrant boundary patterns.*

Your Turn

What follows here is a life reboot that places you squarely on the path to true fulfillment. In other words, it's your turn, my dear. It's your turn to evolve from Boundary Disaster (if you are one) to Boundary Master. And I know you can do it, because I've been witness to many,

many transformations. I've seen the perennial pleaser become a discerning decision-maker, and the exhausted over-giver say no with ease and grace, and so on. As for me, I went from trying to be everything to everyone to focusing my time, energy, and effort on myself and the high-priority people in my life. With my own battle scars in plain sight and my extensive clinical experience, I have created a tried-and-true, step-by-step process to help you overhaul your boundary skills. Now it's your moment to shine.

You've read my story, and you know that the Boundary Boss journey requires some heavy emotional lifting. So, if your self-care regimen could use an upgrade, start now. When I say *self-care*, I'm not talking about planning a spa day or getting a mani-pedi. I mean giving yourself plenty of space and support. For example, instead of pushing yourself to attend an event you'd rather skip, beg off, silence your phone, and simply rest. Experiment with different detox bath recipes. Move your body in restorative ways that feel good, like doing gentle yoga or stretching. Less screen time, more you time. Sit in stillness and silence. You have a butt and a couch— voila! You're a meditator, my friend. Together, we are moving from a modus operandi (MO) of *doing* to an MO of *being*. (At the end of this chapter, you'll create your very own Zen Den, a safe and sacred space for self-care.)

Another word of caution: if you tend toward over-achieving or perfectionism, it's vital not to apply that same hyper-capable approach here or to muscle your way through the Boundary Boss journey. We're not talking about ticking items off a to-do list or resolving dysfunctional relationships in one chapter, because this is a *process*. On the other hand, if you tend to feel overwhelmed or paralyzed when attempting something new, you'll be happy to know that the instructions that follow are simple and the shifts small. This will help keep things manageable.

You also don't need everyone to know that there's a new boundary sheriff in town just yet. No picking up a megaphone and shouting, "Listen, *everyone*, we need to talk." No.

Believe me, I do understand the temptation to march up to Bob in accounting and tell him you're not going to stand for his weirdo comments about your appearance anymore. I know you: you want to get it right. But having tough conversations before you are truly equipped is not the winning formula here. Learning to change deeply ingrained patterns and limiting beliefs takes a minute. Once you fully grasp why it has been so hard to change your behavior and draw better boundaries, then you can approach Bob. Trust me, Bob and his bullshit will still be there when you're ready.

TRUE TALK *There is no one-size-fits-all boundary strategy. You are unique, and so is the right way for you to relate to and express your boundary preferences and deal-breakers.*

As you slowly begin to shift your dysfunctional boundary dance, you can carve out more time for your own true thoughts, feelings, and desires. Along the way, you are bound to bump up against the myth that being *nice* looks a certain way. For example, it might look like picking up your sister's dry cleaning or watching her kids so that she can meet a deadline, even though you'd rather be at yoga, reading a book, or going to see a play. Or not sharing with your partner that you actually do not want to spend every weekend with his/her/their overbearing/lovely/psycho family. Or not going grocery shopping because you're too busy drafting a detailed life plan for your bestie who just got laid off (and, by the way, is not asking for your PowerPoint on how to save her career). Or avoiding the conflict you fear will come from telling a well-meaning pal that you simply don't want her advice.

TRUE TALK *You write the instruction manual on how you treat yourself (internal boundaries) and how others treat you (external boundaries).*

Right about now, you might be thinking, *What's wrong with being nice?*

Real talk: any time you opt for being fake-nice instead of being truthful, you're setting yourself up for unsatisfying experiences, resentment, and the loneliness of not being authentically known. Think about it: is it really "nice" to essentially lie to the people you love and respect by saying yes when you want to say no? Nope. It's just providing them with bad intel and setting yourself up for more of the same.

Creating and maintaining healthy boundaries is a life-changing art. The main driver of this transformation is your *true* feelings. We may tell ourselves that we're being kind in our attempt to spare someone else's feelings, but this is not the whole story. The motivator for these less-than-honest gestures is usually fear, not love, a concept we'll delve into more in chapter 3. Under the guise of being caring, we may find ourselves over-giving, over-functioning, and overextended. Or rigidly refusing all assistance so as not to bother anyone. Both lead to feeling less loved, not more.

When you can speak directly and honestly, the benefits are two-fold. You get to be seen, and you create the space for everyone else in your life to be seen as well. You are no longer robbing the world of your authenticity, something you and only you have.

Healthy boundaries are generous *and* efficient. When they're in place, you will be amazed at how much time, energy, and bandwidth you have for other, more productive pursuits like, say, doing Zumba, learning pottery, or studying quantum physics. Kicking self-abandonment, deceit, denial, and resentment to the curb allows you to create a life based on joy, freedom, and genuine intimacy.

Really, once you become aware, it's an obvious choice, not to **mention** better for everyone.

In many ways, I feel like I already know you because I *was* **you.** Trust me when I tell you that it doesn't matter where you are on **your** Boundary Boss journey or what you do and don't already know. **You** are in the exact right place to start now. As Marianne Williamson once wrote, "It is not too late. You are not too old. You are right **on** time. And you are better than you know."

▶ BOUNDARY BOSS IN ACTION ◀

At the end of each chapter, I'm offering selected exercises for you to incrementally build the foundation of your Boundary Boss skills. Every new thought or action is significant, no matter how small. For even more exercises and support, check out the Boundary Boss Bonus Bundle at BoundaryBossBook.com/bonus.

1. **Top of Mind.** Pay attention to your feelings. As emotions come up, stop to name them. Be mindful that *forbidden* emotions from childhood can be harder to identify and may seem like something more acceptable. For example, my forbidden anger masqueraded as sadness. Use your awareness to recognize and name your true emotions. Then, honor them.

2. **Go Deeper: Make Your Own Zen Den.** Your very first exercise is setting up your sacred space to use throughout our shared BB journey (and beyond) to meditate, rest, journal, and complete your integration exercises. This is your first BB act of radical self-care. It will also help you commit to the process of becoming a Boundary Boss. See page 237 in the "Go Deeper" section at the back of the book for step-by-step instructions.

3. **Get Inspired: Get Your Meditation On.** Meditation increases your mindfulness and strengthens your ability to be in the present moment, which is crucial to successfully becoming a Boundary Boss. Go to page 238 in the "Go Deeper" section at the back of the book for a simple mediation to get started.

CHAPTER 2

Boundary Basics

YEARS AGO, ON A SUNNY SPRING DAY, my pal Jules and I were having a catch-up lunch, just shooting the shit about our respective upbringings, waxing philosophical about why we'd made certain life choices. While sharing what it was like to grow up as one of seven siblings, Jules casually said, "We had a basket on the bathroom counter where we kept all of the toothbrushes."

I was incredulous. "How did you know which one was yours?"

"I didn't," she said, shrugging. "We all just used whichever one wasn't wet."

Wait. What?

I knew that Jules had grown up in a chaotic family fueled by addiction, poverty, and abuse. As a therapist, I'm not fazed by much. Yet something about the specificity of her not having her own toothbrush stopped me cold. That Jules thought it was no big deal was telling, too. She didn't even know she had a right to her own *toothbrush*.

But that didn't mean she didn't want one. She used money from her first paycheck from her very first job when she was thirteen to buy a toothbrush and travel case, which she then kept under her pillow, not in the communal basket.

BACK TO YOU:
What's Your Boundary Baseline?

To help illuminate your boundary baseline, read the questions below and check all that apply to you.

▫ Does attempting to draw boundaries by speaking up create feelings of anxiety or dread for you?

▫ When you are paying for a service, do you avoid telling people if you're unsatisfied?

▫ Do you tend to ignore your preferences or needs for too long and then explode in frustration?

▫ Do you have a very specific idea of the way most things should be done and feel frustrated often by the fact that others are clueless?

▫ Do you often feel sad, angry, or resentful that people don't intuit or respect your boundaries?

▫ Do you often fear or avoid speaking up if you disagree with or have a different opinion from the group or person you're with?

▫ Have you created problematic relationships because of not being able to speak authentically, share your preferences, or say no?

▫ Do you often feel offended by or compelled to correct the behavior of others?

▫ If you feel betrayed, do you cut people out of your life or avoid them rather than initiate a difficult conversation?

> ▫ If friends or family have an issue, do you feel compelled to make suggestions or find solutions for them, even if they have not asked for your help?
>
> Each of the questions points to a specific expression of disordered boundaries that can guide you to the areas that need work as we progress on this journey.

This seemingly small example of poor material boundaries in Jules's family of origin represented a greater dysfunction of neglect and abuse. Her parents did not protect her from violent older siblings; they read her journal and didn't allow her (or anyone) to lock the bathroom door. Her privacy, even while in the tub, was often violated. Like Jules, you may have had so-called minor boundary transgressions that you didn't think a whole lot about. But it's important to recognize that all boundary violations have the potential to plant the seeds for future boundary struggles. Bad boundaries are bad boundaries. And for many of my clients, the unhealthy boundary seeds grew into the inability, as adults, to identify, prioritize, or communicate personal wants, needs, desires, or even preferences.

Personal Boundaries 101

Let's start by covering the basics of personal boundaries, so you can better understand why they matter every damn day. Visualize a house with a tall fence around it with signs that read "Keep Out" and "Violators Will Be Prosecuted." We all understand that fence as a clear boundary. The signage spells out specific consequences for crossing the line.

Even though the underlying mechanism is the same, personal boundaries are more complicated than that fence. We can't simply hang up signs and expect others to respect them. Personal boundaries are invisible and therefore need to be established with words (often repeated) *and* actions. Personal boundaries are also unique to each individual, informed by childhood experiences, cultural norms, gender roles, and an array of other factors. There's no one-and-done action (like nailing up a sign) that covers everything.

Personal boundaries are like a guidebook that you create to clearly identify permissible ways that other people may behave toward you. Yup, that means you actually *can* tell a coworker you aren't down with her daily dose of office gossip because you need to focus on your deadlines. Or let your judgy pal know that her snide comments about your weight/appearance/love life are not welcome. Boundary-setting includes a defined response when someone steps over those limits. That means establishing a clear set of consequences for repeat boundary offenders (more on this in chapter 7).

Creating healthy boundaries protects you from emotional harm and keeps your personal dignity intact. Yes, my dear, healthy boundaries help you to live out an essential truth: you are royalty. Treating yourself like the queen that you are means developing an unwavering ability to know, honor, and protect yourself, instead of abandoning yourself. This is important because how you regard and treat *yourself* sets the bar for every other relationship in your life.

TRUE TALK *You may have been socialized to believe that having healthy boundaries makes you selfish, confrontational, and bitchy, but in fact, having healthy boundaries makes you brave and generous.*

Boundary Categories

Boundaries come in five general categories: physical, sexual, material, mental, and emotional. When any of these boundaries are crossed, we're in trouble. Further, boundaries come in three types: rigid, porous, and healthy. Understanding the categories and the types will help you to see where your boundary issues might be so you can start to correct them. Are your emotional boundaries way too porous? Are your mental boundaries too rigid? Where are you flexible and balanced?

The following are personal boundaries that need your attention:

- **Physical boundaries.** Your most basic physical boundary is your body. This includes who has permission to touch you and how, plus how much personal space you require. Someone grabbing you without your permission, using your deodorant (or your toothbrush!), or barging into the bathroom without knocking while you are in the shower are examples of physical boundary violations.

- **Sexual boundaries.** You get to decide what level of sexual touch is acceptable, as well as where, when, and with whom it can happen. Someone coercing or forcing you to be sexual with them, making lewd comments, or behaving in any way that is intended to arouse or gratify their sexual impulse without your expressed consent are examples of sexual boundary violations.

- **Material boundaries.** You determine how others may (or may not) access your material possessions. This includes whether you lend your money, clothes, car, or other things to friends or relatives, and under what conditions. For example, what areas of your home, if any, are off-limits to guests? Do you require visitors to remove their shoes or not? Someone using your computer without your permission, taking clothes out of your closet, or leaving garbage in your clean car are examples of material boundary violations.

- **Mental boundaries.** You define your thoughts, values, and opinions. In order to have mental boundaries, you must first know what you believe. Having healthy mental boundaries means that you can listen to others with an open mind, even if you disagree, while holding on to your core beliefs. Someone making demands instead of requests, disparaging your beliefs, or disrespecting your *no* in an effort to get their way are examples of mental boundary violations.

- **Emotional boundaries.** You alone are responsible for your feelings, just as others are responsible for theirs. Healthy emotional boundaries prevent you from giving spontaneous criticism or unsolicited advice. They prevent you from blaming others for how *you* feel and, on the flip side, from accepting blame for emotions that are not yours. Emotional boundaries deter you from sharing intimate details about yourself too soon, taking things personally, or feeling guilty for someone else's issues or negative feelings. Also, if you tend to be super emotional, combative, or defensive, you may have disordered emotional boundaries. Someone who invalidates another person's feelings, tells you how you feel or should feel, or asks intrusive questions is violating emotional boundaries.

Boundary Types

Within each category of personal boundaries, there are three types: rigid, porous, and healthy. If yours are too loose or too tight, that's symptomatic of boundary issues.

- **Rigid Boundaries.** If you have too rigid boundaries, you might
  - not ask for help when you need it,
  - avoid close relationships to minimize rejection,

o   be perceived by others as detached or cold,

o   tend to isolate yourself.

People might describe you as unavailable, closed off, or inflexible. You might have adopted a "My way or the highway!" motto or give off an Ice Queen vibe. Since you don't exactly play well with others, you are more likely to immediately exile offenders rather than tell them how they upset you. A common misconception is that having strict boundaries is equivalent to having healthy boundaries. Not so, people, because being inflexible gets in the way of building healthy relationships the same way being too flexible does.

TRUE TALK   *Contrary to popular belief, super inflexible boundaries are not healthy since they are driven by a fear of vulnerability and can inhibit open, healthy relationships and experiences.*

- **Porous Boundaries.** If you have too porous boundaries, you might

  o   overshare your personal information,

  o   say yes when you want to say no,

  o   find yourself taking on or overly investing in the problems of others,

  o   put up with disrespectful or abusive behavior.

People might describe you as overly accommodating, conflict-averse, or very, very nice. You might give off the vibe of a pushover or a peacekeeper. You are influenced by other people's thoughts, feelings, and problems potentially more than your own. (Like when you're about to hit the gym but a friend calls with toxic romantic drama, and so you stay home, take out your copy of the 1985 self-help classic *Women Who Love Too Much*, and start underlining quotes for your pal to read. Pot, meet kettle.) Maybe your attitude in life is, "As long as everyone else is happy, I'm happy."

- **Healthy Boundaries.** If you have healthy boundaries, you
  - value your own thoughts and opinions,
  - feel comfortable asking for or accepting help,
  - know when to share personal information and with whom,
  - can accept and respect the boundaries of others, including someone saying no to a request.

People might describe you as dependable, trustworthy, or confident. If you have healthy boundaries, others feel safe and at ease in your presence. You keep your word, communicate effectively, and take responsibility for your own happiness. (No emotional blackmail required.) You are not emotionally reactive. For example, when you receive a late-night call from a family member who shares unsettling news, you decide to sit with your feelings about it until morning, instead of sending out an SOS text to your bestie after midnight or springing into action mode because you can't bear feeling helpless. You are capable of managing your emotions.

If you have healthy boundaries, you also have an innate sense of context. You know when certain boundaries are appropriate. What's appropriate with family and friends may not be with coworkers or your boss. For example, if you had a painful breakup, sharing your heartache with your gal pals is appropriate. Sharing the details of your breakup with a subordinate or your boss, however, is not.

Cultivating healthy personal boundaries requires discernment and a long, honest, and probably long overdue look at the state of your relationships, including the one you have with yourself.

It Works until It Doesn't

Jules's quest for her own toothbrush illustrates a natural response to disordered material boundaries. Come hell or high mouthwash, she was going to eke out a corner of the family bathroom that belonged to her and only her.

Throughout her childhood, Jules learned to suppress her feelings, needs, or preferences as a way to avoid being a target of abuse. When her father got drunk, he was violent (physical boundary violation); her siblings helped themselves to her clothes and other possessions (material boundary violation); and she was teased and called "fat and ugly" by her older brothers (emotional boundary violation). From these experiences, she concluded that not making waves and trying to please the people in her life was the safest strategy. Her learned boundary behaviors were adaptive in her childhood situation. But those same behaviors led to conflict and dissatisfaction once she left her childhood home. They became maladaptive. The impact of something as seemingly minor as fighting to have her own toothbrush was, in fact, major.

As an adult, her now maladaptive boundary style (porous) resulted in a decade-long streak of craptastic romantic disasters. Each relationship in some way repeated her disordered boundaries from childhood. Like her siblings, Jules's boyfriends felt entitled to the fruits of her labor, such as her hard-earned cash, her apartment, as well as her time and effort (material boundary violations). She believed loving someone meant doing what they asked and letting them take what they wanted (disordered emotional boundary). She hit a tipping point after her last relationship crashed and burned, realizing, at last, that *she* was the common denominator in these painful experiences. Jules described her role as "always giving." In my opinion, "severely codependent" would also be an accurate descriptor. Relegating her own needs to the sideline had ensured security and love in the dysfunctional dialect of her family's language. However, in adulthood, abandoning herself had become a massive obstacle to her well-being and happiness. Not only that, her disordered boundaries ultimately put her in real danger. She came within a hair's breadth of losing everything.

TRUE TALK *The different boundaries that need your attention are physical, sexual, material, mental, and emotional. Within these categories, your boundaries may be rigid, porous, or healthy.*

A few choice examples from Jules's romantic history reveal echoes of her early material boundary violations. For instance, one time she allowed a new paramour to move in with her because he had stopped being able to pay his rent and was getting evicted. With another ex, she leapt at the chance to design and build the set for his off-off-off-Broadway play, even though she was already working full-time and had no energy to even get herself to the gym. She also eagerly invested more than half of her savings in yet another bad boyfriend's "invention," never to be repaid a penny. You get the picture.

In short, her boundaries, material and otherwise, were *way* too flexible. This sometimes manifested as crippling indecision, which kept her stuck in terrible situations long past their expiration date. Word to the wise: indecision is a common experience for women with disordered boundaries. If your boundaries are too loose (porous), you may fear hurting another person or being rejected or ridiculed for a decision. Indecision can be an unconscious way of avoiding that situation. If you deny yourself the right to change your mind, can't speak up, or say no, every decision carries the weight of a life sentence.

As ridiculous as it sounds, Jules's siblings actually mocked her for wanting her own toothbrush as a tween. They put her down, saying she had become a "demanding diva." (I mean, *come on*.) Like many women, Jules was directly and covertly informed that having healthy boundaries made her selfish, confrontational, and bitchy. Nothing could be further from the truth.

Jules's skewed early understanding of love and security directly translated to her abandoning herself and her best interests as an adult. She had a misguided sense of loyalty, even to those who didn't deserve her devotion. It would take a lot more than a five-dollar dental hygiene purchase at Walgreens to transform the damaging patterns she'd internalized.

Again: the *adaptive* strategy Jules relied on in her earliest years became *maladaptive* in adulthood, setting her up to be used and underappreciated, which is exactly how she felt as a child (no coincidence there). This is what I call a Repeating Boundary Pattern, in which present-day dysfunction mirrors a painful past experience (more on this in chapter 5).

Our Collective Past Informs Our Present

To fully understand personal boundaries, we must acknowledge an even larger context than what we've learned in our family's systems: the history of oppression. The evolution of women's rights directly impacts our conscious, unconscious, and collective relationship to our beliefs about boundaries, even today. Without raising our consciousness about our history, the past can easily become our present.

Think about this fact: prior to the Nineteenth Amendment to the US Constitution in 1920, which gave predominantly white women the right to vote (women of color were essentially restricted by state-specific laws), women were basically the property of their husbands. (Yes, property. Just like land, cattle, or a car. No rights, no sovereignty, no say.) The year 1920 was just over a hundred years ago! Kinda mind-blowing. But, then again, not really.

For hundreds—if not thousands of years—women have been marginalized and objectified. Women of color exponentially more so. Being a part of a marginalized group negatively impacts self-identity and self-worth. According to E. J. R. David, the author of *Internalized Oppression: The Psychology of Marginalized Groups*, we commonly buy into the negative messages about who we are as women, even unknowingly. This is the result of internalizing the experience of oppression, which can lead to feelings of inferiority and self-loathing.

There are a few ways this internalized oppression manifests in women. We invalidate our own experiences, for example, by not speaking up because we fear being seen as drama queens. We become overly concerned with our physical attractiveness, identifying with youth and beauty so much that we believe we are less valuable as we age or if we show signs of aging. We readily prioritize the needs and desires of others above our own, as if self-sacrifice proves that we are "good." Internalized oppression only reinforces our disordered boundaries.

If you are a woman who struggles to set boundaries, understand that your difficulty is connected by an invisible thread to generations of countless women who came before you and also doubted their own value. Your struggle is not happening in a vacuum. And for what? Being socialized as a woman? I call bullshit. But we are *still* dealing with the fallout.

Real social change takes time. Look no further than the #MeToo movement, which was originally established by Tarana Burke in 2006 as a campaign to empower, through empathy, women of color who had been sexually abused. Eleven years later, in the fall of 2017, Burke's campaign was reactivated and reapplied much more broadly during the sexual abuse investigation of Harvey Weinstein, a hugely influential film producer. Long-standing gender inequalities, abuses of power, systemic harassment, and sexual assault—conditions that every woman knows firsthand—suddenly became public discussion around the world. Powerful conversations about how such historically imbalanced dynamics have affected women, personally and collectively, led to decisive action against a slew of abusers. Hallelujah and about friggin' time!

Good news: one year after the #MeToo movement tore through accepted prejudices, US voters added a record number of women (117) and women of color (42) to Congress in the midterm elections (hey, it's a start). But such deep bias does not change overnight. The bad news: gender roles remain ingrained in our collective unconscious; they still dictate how we are expected to dress, act, and speak. We still have work to do.

> **TRUE TALK** *Your personal boundaries are informed by your childhood experiences, cultural norms, gender roles, and an array of other factors.*

In the meantime, individuals like us still need to sort out the overt and covert sexist assumptions, projections, and judgments we have endured and internalized since childhood. Whether or not we are conscious of the impact, these disempowering sentiments can powerfully inform our sense of self in a very negative way. And since time waits for no one, your Boundary Boss journey is imperative *now* for you and the future generations who will be empowered by your transformation. In the wise words of meditation and mindfulness expert Davidji, "We transform the world by transforming ourselves."

Changing the Ending

For Jules, it took hitting rock bottom to wake up to the seriousness of her disordered boundaries. Shortly after a relationship ended, a New York City police detective appeared at her door. "Please come with me," he said.

Heart beating wildly, Jules grabbed her coat and followed the officer to an unmarked police car. At the station, the detective questioned her about a credit card fraud scheme. Unbeknownst to her, the ex had been using Jules's mailing address for his nefarious activities, implicating her.

Jules had been so laser focused on taking care of and pleasing her partner that she was oblivious to what was going on right under her nose. Shaken to the core, she realized how close she had come to disaster—criminal charges and a compromised life!

Happily, Jules's story ends well. After this scary incident, she got herself to psychotherapy and put in the hard work, devoted care, and attention to herself and her boundaries. The result? She updated the *How to Treat Jules* instruction manual and became an expert on herself, proficient in the language of expressing, establishing, and maintaining healthy boundaries. Now a Boundary Boss through and through, she has been happily married to her spouse, Gio, for the past twelve years. They met on an old-fashioned blind date, set up by mutual friends, and Jules joyfully became a "bonus mom" to his two daughters, whom she adores. She says she feels like she hit the family lottery.

That Jules eventually overcame the dysfunction of her childhood is a testament to the fact that it *is* possible to learn healthier ways of interacting. Like Jules, you may be moved to transform your boundary skill set not just for yourself, but to benefit those around you. What I really want you to know, though, is that it's never too late to become what you might have been or who you most want to be. Commit to living the life you desire *now*.

TRUE TALK *Creating healthy boundaries protects you from emotional harm, keeps your personal dignity intact, and strengthens your relationships, including the one you have with yourself.*

▶ BOUNDARY BOSS IN ACTION ◀

1. **Top of Mind.** Pay attention to the different catego-
    ries and types of boundaries. How do they play out in
    your current relationships? Which boundary violations
    (physical, sexual, material, mental, emotional) come up
    the most?

2. **Go Deeper: What's Okay/Not Okay.** It's time to honestly
    assess what's working and not working in all areas of your
    life. Go to page 239 in the "Go Deeper" section at the back
    of the book to complete your full Okay/Not Okay master
    list. This is a core transformation exercise. Don't skip it!

CHAPTER 3

The Codependency Connection

ESTHER, A SUCCESSFUL BEAUTY EDITOR, announced her reason for stepping foot in my office before she even sat down.

"SoIjustneedsomestressreduction," she said in a single breath. From her no-nonsense tone, I could tell that Esther was used to being in charge.

"Nice to meet you, Esther," I replied. "I'm Terri."

Sitting down, she took a deep breath and said, "I mean, obviously, I'm *fine*. I just can't seem to ever relax, and now it's taking a toll on my body. I had to call out from work yesterday for the first time, and I *really* do not have time for this! Can you help me?"

Esther's angst-ridden state was familiar to me as a therapist. Often, clients only seek support when they feel like something's gotta give. They may not be fully cognizant of how disordered boundaries are undermining their best efforts to be happy, healthy, and successful. However, their exasperation, frustration, and pain are unmistakable.

From her get-it-done demeanor, I got the feeling that Esther would have scheduled a marathon weekend of intensive sessions if she could, just so that she could check "therapy" off the to-do list and get back to her fast-clip pace, ASAP. But from personal and professional experience, I knew that we needed to first *slooow* down. That way, we could methodically uncover the root of her stress and explore the coping mechanisms that had helped her survive—until now.

Esther reported that her high anxiety had started manifesting in increasing physical pain from multiple ailments. Notably, she had debilitating headaches and temporomandibular joint syndrome, more commonly known as TMJ, from clenching her teeth while she slept. Which, by the way, wasn't as often as she'd like, because she had also been suffering intermittently from insomnia for the preceding three years. Her recent diagnosis of shingles, a viral-infection that caused a painful rash, had become so excruciating it was interfering with her ability to work. All conditions that could be associated with stress and anxiety, I noted.

As I got to know Esther, I learned that she was an only child who had spent much of her childhood navigating life on behalf of her parents, South Korean immigrants who were not fluent in English. From the time she was a child, adult responsibilities fell on her shoulders. She translated at parent-teacher conferences and at medical appointments. As she grew up, Esther felt pressured to conform to her parents' culturally driven idea of success, which was for her to attend medical school. Now, the more Esther received professional recognition as an editor, the more conflicted she felt inside. She was happy for herself but also disappointed. What meant so much to her would never gain her parents' approval.

Her do-it-all nature was also apparent in her love life. Esther's adoring boyfriend was a semi-employed actor who often let her pick up dinner tabs and sometimes "forgot" to pay her back for his share of the fancy vacations that she researched, booked, and thoroughly planned. After the blush of new love wore off, Esther often found herself being the go-between for her boyfriend and his sweet, needy mother. Sometimes she shrugged off their obvious differences with, "Opposites attract, right?" when in fact, she was *clearly* stressed out and tired of being with someone who wasn't pulling his weight.

Once I got the scoop on Esther, I thought, *No wonder you're feeling physically sick.* For someone like Esther, being unable to perform sparks intense anxiety. Her entire identity was based on how well she could manage her external world. It soon became clear that Esther was a high-functioning codependent.

Unpacking High-Functioning Codependency

Like Esther, many of my clients are successful by societal standards— CEOs, mom-preneurs, and Broadway actors. They strive to be good partners, parents, leaders, and friends. They are over-achieving in every way, guided by a belief that to be worthy means they need to handle it *all*. "Help" is a dirty word unless they're the ones helping. While they are busy doing, doing, doing, they miss one crucial fact: they are completely undoing *themselves* in the process. It's exhausting to just think about, right? Ninety-nine percent of the time, this type of over-functioning is indicative of codependency, a condition where women (though fellas can be codependent, too) are compelled to do things for the people in their lives that those other people should be doing for themselves.

When we hear the term *codependent*, certain negative images come to mind: for example, a weak-willed woman who is always saving the day when her alcoholic spouse can't seem to clean up his act; an enabler who lends buckets of cash to a pal who actually needs to learn to fend for herself; or a woman who makes excuses for her abusive partner because she can't bear to be on her own.

In the early years of my practice, most of my high-achieving, highly capable clients balked when I brought up this term, completely offended. "Are you *kidding* me?" I heard time and time again. "Everyone's dependent on *me*. I do *everything*. I'm the one people come to to get shit done and solve their problems."

To be clear: I do not consider codependent people weak or less than—far from it. Since my clients did not identify with the old-school connotations of codependence, I coined a new term: high-functioning codependent (HFC). To be a high-functioning codependent means to feel overly responsible for the feelings and actions of certain people in your life. It can manifest as over-functioning, over-giving, and automatically offering advice in relationships as an attempt to control outcomes (especially when they're not *your* outcomes). And this hyper-focus on the lives of others dictates that your personal needs and desires get sidelined.

For Esther, an HFC through and through, her physical symptoms threatened to upend her "winning formula" of *just do more*. No wonder she was impatient to hear some magical, stress-relieving tips so that she could check the therapy box as done and get back to business as usual. The prospect of not being able to manage and muscle her way through life, which was basically all that she knew, was terrifying.

The childhood experiences of high-functioning codependents vary. You might have grown up in a chaotic, strict, abusive, neglectful, or substance-addicted family system. You might have been taught to prioritize pleasing others. You might have been parentified, meaning forced into the role of caregiver or saddled with adult responsibilities from a young age, like Esther. These experiences can condition you to anticipate and prioritize the needs of others ahead of your own. One thing is for certain, to become a high-functioning codependent, your childhood was, in some way, dysfunctional, and that leads to these behavioral patterns of over-responsibility that can be tough to break. For HFCs, helping, fixing, doing, and saving are an ingrained, unconscious compulsion.

TRUE TALK *To be a high-functioning codependent means having a dysfunctional behavioral pattern: you feel overly responsible for* *the feelings and actions of others, at the expense of your own desires, needs, and well-being.*

If any of this sounds familiar, celebrate! When it comes to personal transformation, you've got to name the dysfunction to change it. Moments of recognition are vital to your growth and well-being.

At its root, codependency is borne of a primal need to survive, to ensure safety and love. In making yourself helpful or even indispensable, you might be unconsciously attempting to ensure that you won't be rejected. This is a very human instinct. While the underlying causes of codependency are perfectly understandable, seeking security, safety, and love in healthier ways is ultimately what you're after.

Self-awareness is your best tool for detecting when your sneaky, die-hard codependent tendencies are what's motivating you. Otherwise, it's easy to go on believing that you are making conscious choices instead of living out old behaviors that do not serve you. It feels like a *choice* to go pick up a pal who's had a bad fight with her spouse and needs somewhere to stay. It feels like a *choice* to bail cousin Billy out of jail when he gets picked up for public intoxication (again). It feels like a *choice* to get embroiled in your kid's first-grade teacher's domestic drama. But here's the thing: a choice and a compulsion can feel a lot alike, but they are not the same. When it comes to being part of another person's solution, if you can't say *no*, for whatever reason, that's an HFC compulsion.

Hey, BB-in-training, no judgment. Remember, I've been there, too. I have some pretty absurd stories from my own disordered boundaries (thankfully, all now in the past). A few examples: I offered to take a college entrance exam for my cousin; I wrote a philosophy paper for a college boyfriend (and got caught); I paid $600 to get another boyfriend's car out of New York City's impound lot (he got a parking ticket the very next day). All these actions were nowhere near my side of the street, but you know what they say about hindsight. Simply put, codependency is a continual state of being focused on the needs, wants, and problems of others, in order to gain approval, feel worthy, and attempt to control the outcomes.

A major indicator of HFC is feeling overly responsible for *all the things*, as if it has to be you who does whatever needs to be done. You may also believe that if you say no, change your mind, or can't follow through for whatever reason, that something *dire* might happen. This false story stems from a child's fear of failing or disappointing others. Situations can feel very urgent, like life and death are in the balance, even when they're not.

To bring a reality check into sessions with over-functioning clients, I run this scenario by them: You're abducted by aliens tomorrow. What happens? Real talk: the sun still rises and sets. Your friends and family find their way. Your boss delegates your projects elsewhere. The grass continues to grow. Life *will* go on without you tearing yourself apart to do all the things you think you *must* do. You don't need to prove your worth by over-giving. You are worthy simply by virtue of being alive, uniquely and authentically yourself.

Another less obvious indicator of HFC is projecting our unacceptable feelings onto another person. *Projection* is the act of psychologically disowning unwanted traits and feelings by ascribing them to another person. "Why are you so furious?" you may angrily ask your cool, collected partner, when, in fact, you are projecting *your* unacceptable anger onto *them*. It can also show up when you deeply dislike a person but experience them as disliking you. ("I have no idea why Cindy hates me!" Meanwhile, you were rage-texting a pal about her just moments ago.) If we don't talk out our charged feelings, we will consciously or unconsciously act them out. (Or, as I often put it, we can only talk it out or act it out.) The unconscious need to use this confusing defense mechanism will be drastically reduced the more you know, accept, and express your real feelings.

BACK TO YOU:
Are You a High-Functioning Codependent?

There's a very fine line between healthy, caring human behavior and codependency. The latter can limit your potential for intimacy and authentic connection and leave you feeling like there's nothing left for you at the end of the day. Codependency also inhibits your ability to create and enforce healthy boundaries.

This checklist will help you identify codependent tendencies. Do you . . .

- Feel responsible for the choices, outcomes, and feeling states of other people?

- Feel like when something bad is happening to someone else, it's also happening to you?

- Feel a need to be "needed" by others?

- Forego your own needs or wants for the sake of others?

- Draw your sense of self-worth and identity from helping others?

- Need to be a part of the solution to someone else's problems?

- Do more than you're asked to do?

- Do things for others that they can and should be doing for themselves?

- Say yes when you want to say no?

- Cover for others (staying up until 2 a.m. To finish your kid's science project that they "forgot" was due tomorrow)?

- ◻ Make excuses for other people's bad behavior?

- ◻ Harbor feelings of resentment or bitterness from over-giving?

- ◻ Think to yourself, at times, *I can't believe they would say that/do that after everything I've done for them?*

The more boxes you checked, the more codependent tendencies you have. And boundary issues. Don't worry; even if you checked every single box, you are exactly where you need to be. Hey, remember this is a no-judgment zone. You are learning more about yourself so that we can use this key information in part 2 of the book.

Common Behaviors of HFCs

For high-functioning codependents, the autopilot of doing, doing, doing is hard to turn off without awareness. Let's take a look at three major ways codependents express their need for control: automatically giving advice, doing the emotional labor for everyone, and tending toward perfectionism.

Ms. Fix-It

Picture it: A pal is sharing her upset about a recent family drama. Before she can even finish her story, you're scanning your brain for how to make her feel better. You Google resources that apply to her situation. You cannot help but step into the role of helper because you have an intense reaction to her distress, and you *must* deliver the cure to what's ailing her. Do you see what you just did there? You assumed that you know what's best for her, unconsciously trying to control the outcome of a situation that, ultimately, is about your friend, not about you.

Partly, you may jump into situations that aren't actually about you out of guilt. As the pioneering clinical psychologist Dr. Harriet Lerner once wrote, "Our society cultivates guilt feelings in women such that many of us still feel guilty if we are anything less than an emotional service station to others." Perhaps you have such a deeply ingrained habit of worrying about everyone else that you don't even notice that your behavior might be driven by guilt.

Not being aware of the underlying emotions that might be fueling your HFC behavior, especially when you feel compelled to "fix," is pretty common because codependents tend to be cut off from their own internal experiences. So when a loved one (or even someone you barely know) is upset, the impetus to offer up a solution comes from an instinct to avoid conflict and minimize pain, namely *your* pain. What we're really saying is, *Your pain is causing me pain, so I'll tell you what to do in an effort to stop feeling this pain.* Compulsively fixing happens to carry a major side benefit: we get to avoid dealing with our own emotional experiences. Yet the answers you seek and the solutions to your problems are always—and only—within you. Same goes for your friends, family, loved ones, and really, just about everyone else on the planet.

I know all about automatically jumping to fix the issues of others. Years ago, my husband, Vic, had been professionally wronged. Instinctively, I felt that I could help him right that wrong. Without blinking, I felt myself going into full-blown mama-bear protective mode. I researched lawyers and was creating a plan of action. Luckily, I had done enough work by that point that I saw my HFC in action. Not only was I not sticking to my side of the street, but I was also fully attempting to sweep up Vic's side without his permission. I was not actually helping him solve his problem. Even worse, my need to control was making him feel bad about himself.

So I checked in with myself and recognized how I was really feeling: totally helpless. *That* was my side of the street. After I acknowledged my feelings (to myself), I approached Vic and said, "Hey, babe, how can I best support you right now?" He asked me to have faith and let him handle things his way. Eventually, he came to an outcome that was fair and satisfactory (and without lawyers). By quelling my own feelings of discomfort, I was able to witness and appreciate Vic being the calm, effective Pisces that he is. Our relationship got stronger as a result. Not such a bad deal, right?

Resisting the urge to solve the problems of others is imperative for intimacy and healthy relationships to thrive. There are so many ways to respond that don't involve you being the savior. You could say, "What do you think you should do?" Or "I have faith in you. Let me know how I can best support you."

Next time the fix-it urge strikes, try pausing and taking a deep breath. Wait for the urge to pass and listen instead of jumping in with your suggestions.

If you don't, you'll miss out on hearing what's really going on with the other person. You'll miss out on knowing their specific feelings and thoughts because you are too intent on staying comfortable yourself. Yes, it can be very difficult to watch people you care about struggle, but creating space for their unique responses is akin to creating space for *them*. As my pal and coauthor of *The Grief Recovery Handbook*, Russell Friedman, once said to me, "Giving people unasked for advice or criticism robs them of their dignity." Whoa.

Unpaid, Invisible Work

Whether you identify a little or a lot as being an HFC, as a woman you have definitely been burdened by work known as emotional labor. Author Gemma Hartley, who popularized the term in a 2017 article for *Harper's Bazaar*, defines emotional labor as "emotion management and life management combined. It is the unpaid, invisible *work* we do to keep those around us comfortable and happy." My twist on it is this: emotional labor is the unseen and under-acknowledged work that drains the crap out of us. Think: spearheading holiday plans for your family, remembering to buy an end-of-year gift for your child's teacher (when you have a partner who is more than able), always taking on the task of divvying up the check at dinner, even though your capable friends could easily do the simple math.

My favorite success story about dropping emotional labor comes from Maddie Eisenhart, a writer, mother, and wife, whose resentment about how much emotional labor she was doing for her spouse started to interfere with her marriage. One day she had an epiphany: she was stepping in to handle numerous tasks that her partner easily could do, like canceling their dog walker. Her partner is an engineer. Making a single phone call was definitely in his wheelhouse. Eisenhart bought a whiteboard, listed all the tasks that needed to be done (and that she had been doing solo) to keep the boat of their family life afloat. Then, she asked her partner to take responsibility for half of the list. Her partner hadn't been aware of his wife's emotional labor or resentment. While there was some tension at first, Eisenhart decided that momentary discomfort was well worth the long-term benefits of not being perpetually low-key angry at her partner. Ultimately, her strategy to more equitably share the emotional labor with her partner worked to the betterment of their union.

Resentment and other negative feelings are going to crop up as part of any sustained practice of doing for others what they should do for themselves. There's a massive downside to unchecked emotional labor. We all have a limited amount of energy to expend, and if you are leaking all of yours in "service" to others, there is little left for your development. Or for thinking about what *you* really want.

Which is why over-functioning can only lead to one place: bitter-land. And why shouldn't you be bitter? You've trained others to expect your all-access, five-star service, with little left for yourself.

Take the example of my friend Sarah. As her sister was dying from cancer, Sarah stepped in to make sure that her sister had the appropriate help, since the rest of the family lived far away. That's commendable. But, without anyone asking her to, Sarah took things to the extreme. In addition to the round-the-clock care she was providing, she also kept her family informed and played therapist to her sister's friends, who were understandably devastated. Sarah didn't even think about all the emotional labor she was doing (nor the energy she was leaking) until one of her sister's friends said, "It's extraordinary. Not only are you taking care of her, but you're taking care of the rest of us, too."

TRUE TALK *Human beings are hardwired to avoid social rejection, a survival instinct that can unconsciously fuel common, fear-driven high-functioning codependent (HFC) behaviors, such as over-giving and not speaking truthfully.*

That was Sarah's light-bulb moment: *Holy crap! If I expended this much energy on my own life, I could be running a multimillion-dollar empire.* It was then she realized that she had gone way beyond her limits. I would characterize Sarah's brand of emotional labor as *auto-accommodating*. She was going out of her way to do things that others didn't even expect of her (whereas in other family systems, emotional labor is often expected). After her epiphany, she began to modify her behavior so that she could make more conscious choices and focus on enjoying the time she had left with her sister.

Perfectionism

Perfectionism is a sanctioned drug in our hyper-ambitious, money-centric society. As such, perfectionism rarely gets acknowledged as the deeply debilitating problem it is. We're so into being busy and successful, to the point of our being workaholics. I had a client who defended her never-satisfied, perfectionistic ways, which included working crazy long hours, by saying, "Well, it's better than being an asshole." Okay, yeah, we can all agree that perfectionism is preferable to being a shitty human. However, that rationale glosses over the immense cost of living by the rigid, fearful code of *Only if I do it all and do it just right will I be happy, worthy, and lovable.*

BACK TO YOU:
Are You a Perfectionist?

Take a minute right now to assess your level of perfectionism. Check the boxes that apply to your behaviors and attitudes:

◻ Super Critical: you are highly critical of yourself and others.

◻ No Pain, No Gain: you consider your workaholism a badge of honor and believe it is necessary to achieve success.

◻ Stress to Impress: at a young age, you learned that your achievements would produce positive feedback, but the desire to excel got tangled up with the fear of failure. It can be an endless cycle of stress.

◻ Death to Mediocrity: your fear of being average drives your need to be perfect. If your success in a chosen endeavor is not guaranteed, you'd rather not try.

□ All or Nothing: you actually fear taking risks because of your need to be the best, which limits your willingness to learn.

□ Rejection Protection: because of your intense fear of rejection and failure, you have a hard time sharing yourself authentically with others.

□ Past Is Present: you regularly replay past failures in your mind and torture yourself with what you "should have" done instead of accepting that you did your best.

□ Everything Is Personal: you are highly sensitive to perceived or actual criticism from others. There is no "constructive criticism"; according to you, anything remotely critical feels like an attack.

□ The Shame Game: you are plagued by guilt and shame for any perceived failures or missteps.

□ Analysis Paralysis: you overthink things to avoid failure to the point of extreme procrastination.

If you checked five or more items on this list, then you have a tendency toward perfectionism. The process of becoming a Boundary Boss is not linear; this intel can assist you through the messier twists of our journey together and remind you to be gentle with yourself. Go easy!

Perfectionism is different from striving for excellence, because perfectionism is the unrealistic and unrelenting belief that you (and others) can and should do and say everything exactly right. It often goes hand in hand with high-functioning codependency because both are rooted in childhood experiences of growing up in an unpredictable, authoritarian, or chaotic environment. The child's *magical thinking* is that if you are perfect enough, you can stop bad things from happening (a parent's relapse or job loss) and avoid criticism, rejection, or worse. In childhood, that unconscious strategy may indeed have driven you to become an honor student or a star athlete, but having unrealistic expectations for yourself and others in your adult life inevitably leads to frustration, disappointment, and boundary conflicts.

Remember: we are still in the awareness-raising portion of our Boundary Boss journey. As these habitual behaviors become conscious, you can turn your gaze inward (meaning, keep your focus on your side of the street). Your struggles with emotional labor, fixing, perfectionism, and other HFC behaviors *can* be the foundation for your superpowers, love. There's just one caveat. You *must* establish healthy boundaries to protect your gifts, talents, sensitivity, and life, so that you are making conscious choices about how you spend your precious time and energy.

Fight-Flight-Freeze, Or How We Learned to Survive

High-functioning codependents may find themselves believing they are acting out of love, when in reality, their dysfunctional behavior may be driven by fear. For one reason or another, many high-functioning codependents learned in their early life that to receive love, nurturing, or approval, they needed to do more than just be a kid.

Like Esther, all of us have unique family and cultural influences that impact our ability to speak truthfully, establish appropriate boundaries with others, and ultimately create lives that we love. Regardless of our cultural background, all of us are *Homo sapiens*, descended from cave dwellers for whom rejection from the pack could mean death. As such, our primal instincts for survival are hardwired into our DNA. Often, this primal fear clouds our judgment and prevents us from seeing life as it really is. Or even how it could be. We're too busy (unconsciously) hoping we don't get rejected/annihilated.

In addition to being hardwired to avoid rejection, a related survival instinct is the fight-flight-freeze (FFF) response, our body's built-in automatic system to protect us from perceived threats (like, say, a pack of wild animals or a hostile tribe). Thanks to this response, as soon as we perceive potential danger, cortisol and adrenaline are released into the bloodstream. Our breathing speeds up to increase oxygen intake. Our pupils dilate to let more light in to better spot the danger. Blood flow is diverted from the stomach and extremities to the larger muscles of thighs and arms in preparation to fight, run away, or hold very still. It's an exquisite system of self-protection, and very useful if the danger is actually life-threatening. But the likelihood of being attacked by a saber-tooth tiger while walking around your neighborhood is exactly zero, so the question becomes: What happens when fight-flight-freeze is still our unconscious go-to, making us walk around like we are in imminent mortal danger, even though we're not? Apparently, plenty.

Author and therapist Harper West has noted that in modern times, fight-flight-freeze is more common in response to emotional threats, like, say, rejection, criticism, and judgment from others. Because human beings are social creatures, the idea of being spurned in interpersonal relationships and interactions carries a profound weight. That weight translates to imagined life-threatening danger and living in states of chronic fear and hyper-vigilance. According to Harvard Medical School, repeated activation of the stress response takes a toll on physical health. Research suggests that chronic stress contributes to high blood pressure, among other conditions, and causes brain chemistry changes that may contribute to anxiety, depression, and addiction.

We each have a unique relationship to stress, which for some people means their body overreacts to relatively harmless situations, like being stuck in traffic or embroiled in relationship or work conflicts. We all have that friend (or family member) who is constantly catastrophically projecting into the future, assuming and preparing for the worst, even though the horrible, terrible thing has only happened *in their mind*. But their body missed the fake-danger memo and released the stress hormones anyway. In many instances, fear becomes a habit, an automated response, even when it's not warranted. That's because the ferocity of such hardwired emotional responses can override common sense.

Good thing we can do something about that. You can put the brakes on this unconscious stress response with raised awareness and solid, daily wellness-boosting routines. Good sleep habits, physical exercise, and mindfulness practices, such as meditation and breathing techniques, can mitigate physical symptoms. You might be shocked by the powerful calming effect of a simple five-minute breathing exercise.

Healthy daily habits also create mental clarity. This is crucial since continuous stress compromises our ability to assess situations accurately. For example, when activated, you may yell at your best friend when a direct conversation would do (fight). Or you may sneak out of a conference early because you dread making small talk (flight). Or if Bob in accounting says something inappropriate, your mind might go blank (freeze). This hyper-vigilant state of self-protection is very common for women and can be a significant block to creating functional boundaries. (We'll explore an effective technique to overcome the freeze response in chapter 9.)

In all of these situations, we are less likely to speak up if our fear of rejection (also known as fear of death) is greater than our desire to be known. And understandably so: breathing trumps being understood.

This acute stress response can also create resistance to becoming consciously aware.

BACK TO YOU:
4 x 4 Breathing Technique

Here's a breathing technique that I use all the time. It takes mere minutes to complete, so you can do it anywhere to create an instant sense of calm. Take a minute to learn it right now. It's easy breezy.

Here's how to do it:

1. Sit comfortably in a chair with your hands on your lap, facing up.

2. Breathe in for four counts.

3. Hold for four counts.

4. Breathe out for four counts.

5. Hold out for four counts.

6. Repeat this pattern until you've completed four rounds.

Ahhhh! That's better. Use this quick stress-relieving practice anytime you need it.

For example, I had a client, Beth, a bank teller, who reluctantly went along with her husband's plot to steal money from bank accounts of deceased individuals with no appointed heirs. Though

Beth had never broken the law prior to this poorly thought-out plan, she followed her husband's lead and wound up serving a prison sentence. The threat of her husband's rejection was so great that she had abandoned herself and her morals completely. (File under: Not Okay.) This is an extreme example of how the fear of rejection can drive self-destructive behavior. Ultimately, Beth, like all of us, is responsible for the choice she made, regardless of the unconscious factors that informed said choice.

> **TRUE TALK** *The fight-flight-freeze (FFF) response is our body's built-in protection system, which can be triggered by emotional threats, like criticism, rejection, and aggression, clouding perception and good judgment.*

If you respond to perceived threats with outbursts, stonewalling, ignoring, attacking, or running away, this is going to inhibit your ability to draw boundaries effectively and with transparency. By becoming aware of your dominant FFF response and how it impacts your life, it's easier to align with your best self and exercise your personal agency. Remember: self-knowledge provides real data about where your attention is needed most. In confronting your own fears of rejection and acknowledging where you may fight, flight, or freeze, you start to understand more about why you aren't drawing healthy boundaries in all areas of your life. Establishing and maintaining healthy boundaries is much easier when you are not operating under the unconscious illusion that you're in a fight for your life.

In Esther's case, our work together helped her realize that her parent's disappointment and judgment of her career choice felt like a life-or-death threat. This perceived threat was a substantial contributing factor in the emotional pain that fueled her workaholic tendencies, which in turn exacerbated her physical symptoms. On

HFC autopilot, she unconsciously believed that if she became successful enough in her chosen field, eventually her parents would accept her choice and be proud of her. (Subtext: she wouldn't be booted from the pack, avoiding rejection/annihilation.)

Realizing that there was more to her professional drive than pure career ambition led to a radical shift in perception, which allowed her to examine her fear of failure and rejection. Acknowledging those fears took away their power over her. This gave us an opportunity to start to question some of her limiting beliefs, starting with her assertion that without her parents' approval of her career, she could never be happy. In this revealing session, Esther was energized, relieved, and excited about these new expanded possibilities. *Woooo-hoooooo!*

Over time, Esther saw that she could accept her parents' wishes for her and *still* be happy with the independent choices she made. In fact, she actually felt proud. She became open to the idea that she didn't need the next coveted gig to feel good inside. She recognized that being loving and dutiful did not need to mean total obedience or self-abandonment.

We also gathered valuable information about how she actually felt about her relationship (not that great). As she identified how her fear of rejection had been playing out, especially with her partner, Esther slowly but surely stepped back so she could simply be a girlfriend, instead of girlfriend/stand-in mother/manager.

Effective and Ineffective Communication

At the heart of personal boundaries is the courage to tell the truth. For high-functioning codependents, a large obstacle to truth-telling is being disconnected from authentic feelings, as we discussed above. That's where awareness, which we're building now, comes in. The next piece of that awareness-raising is a mini-primer on communication.

Just as you relate to boundaries based on what you witnessed and experienced when you were a child, you learn how to communicate based on your family of origin's style and culture, too. Different cultures have different agreements (spoken and unspoken) about what is permissible to talk about and what's off-limits.

In my case, I grew up in a WASP-y family that basically didn't talk about anything messy. Tension was often smoothed over with an innocuous statement, like, "Would you like your eggs poached or scrambled?" or "Beautiful day, isn't it?" As a result, a whole lotta feelings got squashed in the process.

Throughout my twenties, I was extremely frustrated when my boyfriend couldn't read my mind. I made quite the leap and assumed his lack of telepathy meant he didn't love me. In reality, though, I was frustrated that *I* didn't know how to express myself fully. So I blamed him, and, being a high-functioning codependent, my resentment piled up quickly. Somewhere along the way, I knew I had to make the decision to communicate better, regardless of what my boyfriend or anyone else was doing. I hope you're ready to make that decision, too. As I like to say (with a nod to Gandhi), "Be the change you want to see *in your relationships*."

In reality, there are only two types of communication: effective and ineffective. If your goal is to have healthy boundaries, effective communication is a tool you cannot do without. Other skills like emotional intelligence, insight, and empathy are important, but effective communication is *numero uno*. Visualize effective communication as the actual bricks and mortar we'll use to build your healthy boundary castle.

Let's start with ineffective communication. Have you ever said, "Sure thing!" while thinking, *Whhhhhhy?* and then sighing, letting your frustrated body language do the talking? As humans, we need to be witnessed and seen. If you can't use direct language (too threatening!) to convey the message, you will find covert ways to do it.

Passive-aggression, the indirect expression of anger, is perhaps one of the most destructive forms of covert communication. Think: door slamming, sarcasm, heavy sighing, eye-rolling, and stonewalling (and also, yes, giving hostile one-word answers). Have you ever traveled to the southern United States? Societally sanctioned passive-aggression is almost its own dialect. For example, adding "bless his heart" at the end of a bitch fest usually means, *He's an idiot/hot mess/addict/derelict/got the emotional IQ of a sneaker.* Growing up in the more direct, "Are-you-freakin'-kidding-me?" Northeast school of aggression, even I can tell that "bless his heart" ain't about blessing anything.

Ineffective communication is indirect. You could be passive, timid, cryptic, or reserved. You could be angry, antagonistic, bullying, or aggressive. However ineffective communication shows up, you're not stating what you want in a manner that can actually be received by the other party. This usually makes others feel, well, mystified, miffed, and misunderstood. When ineffective communication is in play, you run the risk of conversations devolving into a total shitshow of confusion. One or both of you is left feeling like you have to decode the other party's obtuse messages without an encryption key. No one wins.

If you see yourself in any of those scenarios, take heart. No one's communication is 100 percent ineffective or effective. But just like figuring out how to bake a triple-layer chocolate cake, cite a research paper, or dance salsa, effective communication skills can be learned. (If you want a sneak peak, chapter 10 offers real-life scripts to help you feel more confident saying exactly what you mean.)

Effective communication is direct and to the point, leaving no doubt as to what you mean. You're assertive, but not aggressive or passive. Your fears of stating what you want are dialed down, and you can make simple requests. For example, "I'd like to make a simple request that you stop interrupting me, Aunt Milly." You can ask for, say, a day off in a tone that is friendly and cheerful. You're not burying your real request under a million "I'm sorrys" or dancing around the thing that you really want to ask for. You are clear and open to whatever the other party's response might be. Most of all, you're in touch with and able to express your genuine responses to everything that happens in your life, if you so choose.

With effective communication, dialogues must be just that—a two-way street. Learning to listen with presence and interest is *vital*. Pay attention to the needs and perspectives of the other person, instead of just waiting for the moment you can insert your perspective. We all know a *wait-to-talk-er*. They're not really absorbing what you're saying because they're thinking about which gem they can offer up next. Effective communication is contingent upon you knowing how you feel and learning to be responsive, not reactive. Once that happens, life truly opens up in ways you might not have ever expected.

Emerging

During our time together, Esther got more in touch with her real feelings and realized that she had been communicating ineffectively with her boyfriend. She hadn't told him that she didn't always want to pick up the tab, bail him out, or play therapist. Instead, she had become accustomed to expressing her displeasure with hostile eye-rolls, heavy sighs, changing the subject, and not really listening to him when he felt bummed out about not getting a gig.

Since her mind had been hardwired to fix other people's problems, she often interrupted him, stepping in with faux authority. (Esther knew very little about acting.) Unconsciously, Esther had a need to be needed. Her over-functioning and overdoing were fueled by her own discomfort with the unknown and the pain of her self-abandonment.

Once she understood her own behavior, she found expressing herself much easier. Her partner felt uncomfortable with the shift in dynamics (a concept we'll cover more thoroughly in chapter 7). Eventually, though, her ability to become more conscious about her behavior and express her needs clearly created more space for her to respect her beau. Her new MO of controlling less also made room for her boyfriend to step up and take actions that benefitted not only their relationship but his own life as well.

For Esther, becoming an agent of positive changes in her own life created a wide variety of emotions. At different turns, she felt surprised, relieved, frustrated, and hopeful. She compared it to "cleansing the doors of perception," referring to a quote by poet William Blake.

Dropping the safety blanket of high-functioning codependency takes grit, guts, and a desire to be self-determined. (I like to say this work ain't for the weak at heart!) It may feel like a reckoning of sorts. Hey, at least for most of us, it's been a long time coming (like . . . a lifetime).

Speaking your truth Boundary Boss-style may feel like a tall mountain to climb at this very moment. But please know that any fears you might be having are totally normal. The eventual benefit will far outweigh any feelings of trepidation that might come up. In reconfiguring your boundaries, you are creating a whole new Technicolor world. As civil rights activist and poet Audre Lorde once said, "When I dare to be powerful, to use my strength in the service of my vision, then it becomes less and less important whether I am afraid."

Hydrate, take a power nap, and I'll meet you in the next chapter, where we'll delve more deeply into the Bad Boundary Data that's been messing with your boundary mojo.

I got you, babe.

And you got this.

▶ BOUNDARY BOSS IN ACTION ◀

1. **Top of Mind.** Pay attention to when you automatically give advice, feel compelled to fill a lull in a conversation, or communicate indirectly.

2. **Go Deeper: Emotional Labor Assessment.** How much invisible, unpaid, exhausting work do *you* do? Go to page 241 in the "Go Deeper" section at the back of the book to uncover where and with whom you might be doing more than your share of the work.

CHAPTER 4

Corrupted Boundary Data

WHAT WE DON'T KNOW can most definitely hurt us.

That was the case for Rachel, a client who had come to me to figure out why she felt stuck in her life. She worked as a freelance graphic designer for years with a steady stream of clients but often felt like she could be doing more. She had several passion projects in mind, but she couldn't find the time to get them off the ground. Her romantic life consisted of a series of short-term flings that were hot and heavy at the outset, soulmate central until the inevitable spectacular implosion. By the time she was in therapy, she had landed in a toxic, on-off relationship with a man who was not emotionally available to her. He often left town with little warning, usually after they had reached a new level of intense bonding.

She told herself that his distance worked for her. A perfectionist, Rachel believed that she would not be worthy of a relationship until she had reached a higher level of success. That her on-off boyfriend was very wealthy only strengthened her belief (read: panic) that she had to reach a certain financial and professional bar to be ready for an actual commitment. So, if he was not fully there for her, she had time to achieve more financial security. Their emotional connection, she told herself (and me), was enough to sustain her.

She delivered this assessment with confidence. Clearly, she had been working on the spin in her mind for some time.

"How do you feel when your boyfriend goes MIA?" I asked her.

"Upset," she said, looking down.

"What is it like when he returns? Do you tell him how you feel?" I asked.

She shook her head no. She tended to stew, talk about her relationship obsessively with friends, and take six hot yoga classes a week. Then, when she would inevitably see him again, she'd act like everything was fine.

She added, somewhat sheepishly, "But sometimes, when it gets to be too much, I do have emotional outbursts."

She didn't express anger in these moments, but sadness. He was always empathetic, but his behavior never changed. Though she was deeply entrenched in this unhealthy dynamic, she also knew that she needed to change herself. To do so, I knew that we had to go on an expedition of sorts, down to Rachel's basement to peek into the corners and unpack her Boundary Blueprint.

Your Boundary Blueprint

Often, when we are stuck in disordered boundary hell (and yes, it is *hell*), we don't realize that our Boundary Blueprint is driving our adult beliefs and behaviors. Think of your Boundary Blueprint like the architectural blueprint for a house that you did not design.

Unpacking the inherited beliefs that took root in childhood is *critical* in living with full agency. This mostly unconscious material has been informing all aspects of your lived experience, and a lot of the time, not in a good way. Without consciousness-raising and behavioral change, we repeat what we saw and intuited in our earliest years (known as Repeating Boundary Patterns, the topic of chapter 5).

It makes perfect sense, really. Children are always watching, learning, and absorbing information from their environment.

They observe how their parents operate and receive the message loud and clear: *This is how to relate in the world.* That information becomes their baseline for what to believe and how to behave.

As adults, we understand that most parents were doing their best, while also recognizing that our parents' limits and ignorance might have created harmful experiences or beliefs. Even if parents want a better life for their child, they may not have had the tools to make that a reality.

Your parents also unconsciously absorbed a Boundary Blueprint from *their* parents. Boundary Blueprints, like family recipes or traditions, tend to get passed down through the generations. Unexamined, this legacy shapes our present-day lives.

The most important aspect of this excavation process is really grasping *that someone else designed* your Boundary Blueprint decades, or even centuries, ago. Read that last line again, and let it sink in. Many of us are operating on and making boundary decisions based on data from *the olden days.* Yes, my dear, ancient blueprints are fueling your particular brand of boundary and communication challenges right now.

TRUE TALK *Your Boundary Blueprint reflects your early childhood experiences, as well as any inherited family and cultural beliefs that have been passed down through the generations and unconsciously drive your boundary behavior today.*

Understanding Resistance

Rachel was not enthusiastic at the thought of heading into the dusty boxes of her psyche's basement. When I asked about how her parents communicated and drew boundaries, she resisted.

"Well, they didn't do either well, but if I start talking about that, we'll be here for years," she said with an eye-roll.

BACK TO YOU:
What's Your Boundary Blueprint?

Remember the dusty basement? In order to become boundary literate, we must locate the childhood experiences that shaped your blueprint. Bringing hidden material up from the basement (your unconscious) into the main house (your conscious mind) lets you see it and change it.

Let's reflect:

- When you think back to your childhood home, were people allowed to have their own private thoughts, conversations, and relationships?

- Were you allowed or encouraged to express your ideas and feelings, especially if they were different from other members of your family?

- When there was conflict, did members calmly talk issues out or did they scream at each other? Or not talk at all?

Reflecting on these questions creates a quick snapshot of your childhood boundaries. That's helpful. But filling out the big picture in its *entirety* is where it's at. The full Boundary Blueprint exercise is one of the foundational exercises of your Boundary Boss journey. So, when you are finished with this chapter, grab a cup of tea, get snuggled up in your Zen Den, and go for it. You'll find the exercise for going deeper on page 242 at the back of the book.

Before I could guide Rachel in unpacking her boundary inheritance, I needed to show her how connecting the dots from her present-day life would, in fact, be beneficial (and not take years).

We needed to identify the original injury that had planted the **seeds** for her current romantic situation, but first we had to get past **her** Fort Knox–level resistance.

Emotional resistance fuels self-sabotage. I see it all the **time.** Clients come in, enthused by the prospect of change, yet they **stop** short of taking the actions required to achieve their stated **goals.** You might think, *Why would anyone stop taking the actions that are the path to their freedom, happiness, and fulfillment?* Well, emotional resistance helps us avoid the discomfort that conscious personal transformation can provoke. This instinct doesn't make us wrong **or** bad or less than. It simply makes us *human*.

The unknown is scary, and that's exactly what we're facing **when** we decide to transcend the patterns, beliefs, and behaviors that **are** keeping us stuck. So, we use all kinds of rationalizations to **justify** *not* doing the exact things we claimed we wanted to do. For **example,** if you are feeling resistance around establishing healthy **bound-** aries, you might lend your copy of *Boundary Boss* to a friend **you** decide needs this more than you. (Codependency as avoidance— you, sly fox, you!) Or, maybe you get embroiled in drama that **has** nothing to do with you, so that you can put off doing the **thing** you know deep down you should be doing for yourself and **your** own life.

> **TRUE TALK** *Emotional resistance fuels self-sabotage. It is an unconscious way that human beings avoid the discomfort that conscious change and personal transformation can provoke.*

Understanding Secondary Gain

With Rachel's resistance so deeply entrenched, I sensed that **help-** ing her get unstuck would require more than encouraging her **to be** curious about her feelings. We had to identify her *secondary gain*, **or** how she "benefitted" from self-sabotaging resistance.

After a month, I said to her, "I'm going to ask you a question that might sound counterintuitive, but indulge me. What are you getting by staying stuck in this dynamic of not confronting your boyfriend about his disappearing act?"

Rachel stared blankly at me. *Huh?*

"Let me be more specific. What do you get to *not* feel, face, or experience by staying stuck in this pattern?" I asked.

Rachel thought about my question for a moment and replied, "Well, I get to avoid having conflict. I get to avoid feeling awkward in bringing up a conversation I really don't know how to have."

Clearly, Rachel didn't want to be vulnerable, which is exactly what speaking honestly with her boyfriend would require. She felt ill-equipped to ask him why he would drop out of sight for days or weeks and then reappear as if nothing happened. So, in essence, she was saving herself from the pain of facing her feelings of being unimportant or discarded. My sense was that this pain mirrored the unexplored pain of her childhood.

Secondary gain is the *unobvious* gain we receive by staying stuck in unhealthy patterns of behavior. With primary gain, the benefit to a certain action is apparent, like going to the gym to get an endorphin rush. Secondary gain, though, operates on a far more covert level and is usually unconscious. For example, a woman in a loveless marriage might continue her nightly "wine therapy" habit (even though it makes her feel miserable the other twenty hours of the day) to numb feelings of despair and hopelessness. All the effort in the world won't help you to move forward until you can become aware of, and explore, how you "benefit" from dysfunctional behaviors or, more specifically, what feelings and experiences the secondary gain guards against.

Not surprisingly, secondary gain is one of *the* main reasons that people stay stuck in dysfunctional relationships, as well as unhealthy boundary and communication patterns. Fortunately, illuminating your secondary gain can help you move out of resistance and into conscious Boundary Boss action.

> **TRUE TALK** *Asking yourself what you get to not feel, face, or experience if you stay stuck will reveal its hidden benefit. Asking this question is a powerful tool for moving past resistance.*

This was definitely true for Rachel. Once she started to see how her stuckness was working for her, she felt some relief. She admitted that she'd been beating herself up about her situation, feeling as if there was something deeply wrong with her for being in this relationship, which she knew, on a common-sense level, was not good for her. Knowing that she wasn't the only human being alive trying to protect herself in this ass-backwards way made her feel more compassionate toward herself. That small victory was so not small, people.

Pain is *the* single greatest motivator for change, so if your secondary gain is covertly protecting you from pain, guess what? No impetus for change.

Socially acceptable levels of drinking, workaholism, or over-exercising (behaviors I refer to as *shadow addictions*) often impede personal growth but serve the secondary gain of avoiding emotional pain. Such behaviors numb the feelings we really don't want to feel. Though shadow addictions might not lead immediately (or ever) to the disastrous outcomes that full-blown addictions tend to, they foster emotional confusion instead of emotional clarity, and that blocks our growth. Besides dulling the pain that could motivate us to draw healthy boundaries, eventually these dysfunctional behaviors will create distraction pain (like poor health or booze-fueled drama) that co-opt our bandwidth and drain our energy. Not a whole lot of psychic space to enter your basement when you're constantly putting out the fires you unconsciously set to distract yourself from the real issue.

TRUE TALK *Shadow addictions are behaviors that numb our emotions and create distractions that keep us in familiar dysfunctional patterns and behaviors.*

With therapy, Rachel became more conscious of her secondary gains, as well as her shadow addiction to hot yoga, which she'd attended pretty much *no matter what* (even on days when heat advisories were in effect). Now we were getting somewhere.

Back to the Basement

Heightened awareness cracked the cellar door for Rachel. Slowly, she began to open up about what she witnessed and experienced as a child. Her father, a well-respected lawyer, controlled the finances, which gave him more power in her parents' relationship. Her mother, as a result, was often begging for basic support like groceries or school clothes for the kids. This money/power struggle happened daily, with her mother pleading her case for how much she needed every morning before her father left for the office. Rachel remembered thinking, *That will never be me.*

The brewing conflict exploded when Rachel's mother brought her to her father's office and began making a scene in front of her father's clients. "We need carpeting at home! How could you get new carpeting here but not for your own family?" she screamed.

Her mother's out-of-control emotions were so intense that clients were asked to leave. But when the whole family gathered for dinner later, all her father said was, "Delicious pork chops, dear."

No one said a word about the loud confrontation from earlier in the day. Or the carpeting, for that matter. That lack of acknowledgment can lead children to internalize the dysfunction and also sometimes wonder if something must be wrong with *them*, since the parents act like their dysfunctional behavior is normal or didn't happen.

This snapshot from Rachel's early life spoke to a greater pattern of how her parents were ill-equipped to handle conflict or to problem-solve effectively. Their model of ignoring, denying, and then exploding is common in families where there is abuse, addiction, or straight-up ineffective communication.

Many families offer their children some pretty bad data on interpersonal boundaries. As a result, children learn, *This is what people do. This is what I'm supposed to do.* As adults, we unwittingly build our lives and relationships on this corrupted intel.

Once we accessed the subconscious material in Rachel's basement, it was easy to see why the situation with her boyfriend felt so familiar to her. Delving into the more difficult parts of her childhood was painful. But after realizing that continuing to stay stuck would be way more painful than facing the truth, Rachel allowed herself to cry buckets, in my office and at home.

Her tears brought clarity. Like her mother, she was not getting her needs met and occasionally resorted to emotional outbursts, which did nothing to change her boyfriend's behavior. Her mother's secondary gain in avoiding healthy conflict was that she didn't have to risk raising her children alone with no resources. Like her mother, Rachel let *way* too many things slide out of fear and then erupted when stifling her emotions became intolerable. Like her mother, Rachel felt helpless and had ignored her boyfriend's shit behavior because she felt disempowered, especially with the financial disparity in their relationship.

TRUE TALK *By examining your Boundary Blueprint, you can upend established, unconscious dysfunctional patterns to consciously create a better blueprint for relating to yourself, others, and the world.*

Now that Rachel understood more about her Boundary Blueprint, she was excited and ready to mindfully craft a new one, based on a future she wanted, not her family's past.

Sneaky Boundary Blocks

Now that you are familiar with Boundary Blueprints, let's take a look at some of the most common ways dysfunctional boundary behavior patterns manifest in everyday life.

Do You Have a Velvet Rope on Your VIP Section?

Take a minute to think about who you go out of your way for, rearrange your schedule for, and try to please. And more importantly, ask yourself why?

Your VIP section represents that sacred place in your heart, mind, and life and is (or should be) reserved for those connections that add value—to enliven, nourish, and energize you. Truth: not just anyone deserves to be there! In VIP-worthy relationships, there's mutuality, respect, and healthy compromise. Your VIPs don't have to be perfect. They're human, like you, but they certainly should not leave you feeling constantly drained, used, or abused.

If you suffer from the disease-to-please, though, you may have been influenced by an unconscious blueprint that mandated that all family members *must* be allowed access to your VIP section. Or friends from grammar school. Or ex-lovers. Or frenemies. Or basically *anyone* who believes they belong there. So you have no bouncer, no rope, and probably no inner peace, either.

Some people feel entitled to 24/7 access, and if you suffer from high-functioning codependency, setting them straight, directly, is not your default response. Maybe you have a friend who calls for your grade-A comfort (day or night) every time something in her life goes awry. You listen begrudgingly while your stomach is in knots and later tell someone who actually *is* a VIP, "I can't believe she called me so late again! Who does that? Why?"

Really, though, who cares why she called for the millionth time? We should not be concerning ourselves with the *whys* of others.

After all, people *can* and *will* ask and expect ridiculous shit from us. That's not your problem unless you make it so. Focusing on them is only a distraction. Put your attention back on yourself.

Becoming a Boundary Boss means getting really curious about your own *whys*. In this case, the real question is, *Why do you keep picking up the phone?*

Your VIP section is based on your values, your integrity, and your deal-breakers. If you have a shady, law-breaking friend and honesty and integrity are important to you, ask yourself: *Does this person qualify for my VIP section?* The answer is probably gonna be no.

You may grapple with oppressive ideas of loyalty or familial devotion, which is normal. But if Mom/Dad/sister/whoever hasn't earned your trust or respect, you have the right to draw a line. In fact, you have an obligation *to yourself* to ensure that no one gets beyond the velvet rope without your express permission.

Please understand: when you have healthy boundaries, you actively make the distinction between higher and lower priority people. This might sound cold, but, real talk, it's not possible or appropriate for everyone in your life to be a high priority. Does spending time with someone energize or deplete you? Do you look forward to it or secretly kinda dread it? What relationships feel like an obligation rather than a choice? The answers to these questions should inform the amount of access you permit to you, your life, your energy, and your precious time.

Listen, you don't have to make any big decisions right now (or ever!) if you don't want to. My goal is for you to get crystal clear that *you* decide who gets the distinct privilege of being in your life. You can prune your VIP guest list any time you choose. Whether relatives, friends, or demanding colleagues, you don't need to dramatically excommunicate anyone, unless you want to. Part of the Boundary Boss journey means shifting away from the mindset of the conditioned self (*If I don't include my cousin in my birthday plans, she'll be so upset*) to the mindset of the empowered, developing self (*Who are the important people I want to spend my birthday celebration with?*). Point is, you have choices, and if letting your cousin crash your birthday soiree will make you feel put-upon, then don't include her.

Do You Always Say Yes?

Do you give from a place of conscious choice? Or is "Sure thing!" your default response? If it's the latter, you're likely saying yes automatically. Anything automatic is a reaction, not a mindful choice. I call this the Insta-Yes. Maybe you were asked to organize your kid's class fundraiser, and even though you're in the midst of a move or your mother is sick and you really, really don't have time to collate packets, or do whatever is required, you say yes anyway. As if you don't even have a choice.

Saying yes without much thought is the result of lifelong conditioning. You may feel like a pushover, or perhaps others see you that way. Usually, though, you most likely knew in the moment, somewhere down deep, that you should have declined.

Stopping the Insta-Yes is easier than you might think. Practice interrupting this habit by inserting a moment of silence instead.

While allowing a moment of silence might feel like not calling the fire department when the house is burning down, in reality, you *deserve* that time. (And PS: there's no actual fire.) You owe *no one* your immediate yes—or even your delayed yes. A pause and then a simple "I'd like to think about it" can be a useful response. You will be amazed at how liberated you feel by not automatically agreeing to something that is counter to your real feelings.

In this example, buying time interrupts the ingrained pattern, which helps create space to think about what you really want and how you really feel. Try it! By any means necessary, we gotta *stop* doing a ton of optional crap we don't really want to do. That allows us to show up fully to things we actually *do* want to do.

You can experiment with the empowering use of silence in other ways, too. Instead of feeling like it's your job to fill in awkward silences, you could view these moments as *power pauses*, which have the potential for you to connect more authentically. Talking to avoid an awkward silence might be preferable in the moment, but it's also a lost opportunity for deeper connection and intimacy (and not the way of a true BB). If you set your intention to allow for some moments of silence, you may be pleasantly surprised at how much you learn about both the people in your life and yourself.

TRUE TALK *Dysfunctional boundary patterns include the inability to make discerning choices about who belongs in your VIP section and automatically accommodating others before considering your own needs, desires, and feelings.*

Do You Over-Give?

Over-giving is the evil stepmother of the Insta-Yes. If you are an over-giver, you feel like it's your duty to give until you can't give any more. If you are a high-functioning codependent, then you definitely know what we're talking about here: volunteering for all the things, going out of your way to send a gift basket to a coworker in the midst of a health crisis, offering to help with a professional task that is not your responsibility—but hey, you sense that someone needs help, so it might as well be capable you to the rescue.

You don't have to identify as a high-functioning codependent to fall into this disordered boundary trap, though. We have been indoctrinated as women to be a particular way in the world. If we were really good moms, good sisters, good daughters, good *everything-to-everyone*, then we would be selfless. We would deal with whatever anyone decides to put on our plate and also insert ourselves, often inappropriately, under the guise of giving and niceness. As a recovering over-functioner and over-giver, I really get it. Putting others' needs above our own is what supposedly makes us good people, right? Turns out, that thinking is just wrong.

The next time you feel the urge, ask yourself, *Am I giving from a place of love or a place of fear or need?* As put-together as you may be, you might resist thinking of yourself as fearful or needy. However, in many cases, that's precisely what lies underneath the smooth, genteel surface of this kind of so-called generosity. Maybe the fear is about being perceived as insensitive or the need is about *you* feeling good, calm, and in control. By becoming indispensable, you might also find a sense of security.

If you continue on this path for long enough, though, the "nice" sheen wears off. You'll eventually start to feel resentful and maybe even *freaking done* with the entire human race. *Selfish users that they are!* (I'm kidding here, but resentment can sound a lot like this.) It's actually common to blame the other person for their entitlement as a way of avoiding getting our own boundary house in order. We have to remember: giving is loving; over-giving is dysfunctional.

Over-giving and codependent behavior eventually lead to feeling empty because at the end of the day there's nothing left for you. Are you really a constructive problem-solver if your blanket solution to life is *I'll do more?* Nope. Because no one can do that forever.

The way out of this hellacious, self-sabotaging trap is mindfulness plus self-care. To interrupt these ingrained patterns, consider yourself first, instead of giving to others first. Consider checking in with yourself before committing. Base every decision on your available bandwidth, how you feel, and whether the person is a VIP or not. You can do this. It will take practice, but you definitely can. And in doing so, you will recalibrate your generosity meter, so that giving will feel good and be authentic.

Do You Agree Now, But Resent Later?

Have you ever agreed to do something with or for a loved one or colleague, and then as soon as you walked away thought, *Crap, why did I just say I would do that?* This is a setup to be resentful later. It is a short-term strategy to avoid discomfort that produces long-term problems.

Here's a textbook example. I once had a client from a poor Midwestern farming family who was about to wed a wealthy Manhattan real estate mogul. She was genuinely smitten, but his family was not happy. They cast her in the unflattering role of a gold digger. Aware of how they felt, she instantly agreed to sign a pre-nuptial agreement with terms highly unfavorable to her. "I'm sure it's going to be fine," she said to me. Oh, it was not fine. Not at all.

Ten years, three kids, and several affairs (on his part) later, his family's prayers were answered: the marriage imploded, and she wasn't protected. She lost her home, alimony, and most of their shared "friends." Why? Because she decided to attempt to make his family happy by signing the prenup instead of taking care of her own interests. She did it in the naïve hope that they would eventually see her good intentions and come to love and accept her, but that never happened.

Often, when agreeing in the moment, we allow ourselves to be pressured, not realizing (or even half-realizing) that we might end up feeling pretty pissed off down the line. This type of agreement is sometimes driven by a fear of appearing selfish. We undercut our own interests thinking we'll be better liked or better leveraged if we do.

My client did not want to appear greedy, and so she signed that prenup. People, we need to seriously rethink this outdated, approval-seeking, self-abandoning behavior. A woman who takes care of herself, prioritizes her thoughts and feelings, and knows a terrible deal when she sees it is a Boundary Boss. And that is a good thing.

Do You Refuse Help?

"No worries, I got it." If this is a familiar refrain, you may be blocking help, even when it is freely and sincerely offered. Asking for help, even if you really need it, is a worst-case, last-resort scenario for most of my high-functioning codependent sisters. If you have an automatic "Nah, I'm good" response for most things, it's time to check yourself.

I know this habit well. When I started dating my husband, Vic, I was used to doing everything for myself (and then some). From the beginning of our courtship, he consistently offered to do nice things for me, like getting our opera tickets before coming to pick me up, so I wouldn't have to wait in line in the rain. Every time he offered something considerate, I'd say, "Oh, don't worry about it." I could not for the life of me understand why he seemed so disappointed. Then my mother caught wind of this and asked me, "Why are you denying Vic the joy that taking care of you brings him? He doesn't *have* to do any of those things, Ter. He *wants* to."

Huh. Never thought of it that way.

She added, "Imagine his offers as wrapped gifts, and every time you say no, it's like throwing a gift back in his face. Please learn from me. If you never ask for or accept help and insist on doing everything yourself, eventually the offers stop coming, and you will end up like me, doing it all alone."

Damn.

Mom's truth-talk hit me like a punch in the gut, and from that moment on, I began accepting and allowing help from Vic, and others, too. (Thanks, Mom.)

Your job as a BB-in-training is to start to become conscious of why you are automatically declining offers or not requesting assistance. Ask yourself, *Why am I not saying yes? Why am I not asking for what I need? What am I afraid of?*

Often, declining help is a covert way of maintaining control. You may not want to feel like a burden, indebted, or risk being vulnerable. This can show up in ways both large and small. You may be so committed to self-reliance that you don't even let a cab driver help you put your heavy bags in the trunk on the way to the airport.

Or you may find yourself in the midst of a family health crisis or work drama and simply hole up, taking care of everything for and by yourself. But here's the thing, healthy vulnerability (or voluntary vulnerability, which we cover in chapter 6) is the foundation for authentic intimacy. So raise your awareness around all the ways, big and small, that you might be blocking people from adding value to your life. You deserve to be intimately known and supported.

Do You Do That Hyper-Positivity Thing?

Have you ever shared something painful with a pal, and no matter what your feelings or tone, she'll reply with a version of "well, everything happens for a reason"? Ugh. That is an example of hyper-positivity, where you or others respond to news that's unsettling or uncomfortable with a forced explanation (like above) or a chirpy affirmation like, "This too shall pass."

Thanks for nothing, Betty.

Don't get me wrong. Having an authentically optimistic outlook on life raises your energetic vibration. It is one of the most powerful tools I use to be happy in my own life. But using positivity to "fix" what the other person has shared is bad listening and not your job.

Hyper-positivity is a form of denial, a refusal or an inability to face reality. It's used when we don't really want to deal with uncomfortable feelings. Anyone who has ever been through divorce, illness, or any other kind of crisis has likely encountered hyper-positivity in others' responses to their situation. When I received my first cancer diagnosis, a pal said, "Well, this is a good opportunity for you to explore your shadow self." *Not exactly my go-to response to this health crisis*, I thought. *But thanks for your unsolicited two cents.* Though I wasn't opposed to doing shadow work, I was put off by her insistence on hijacking the narrative of my story so that *she* could feel some semblance of control.

It can be upsetting to be on the receiving end of intrusive hyper-positivity. Just know that anyone who employs it (and this includes you) is clinging to this distorted, avoidant, self-protection mechanism because they don't have the capacity to sit with pain or discomfort.

Learning to draw boundaries with ease and grace and honoring yourself by speaking authentically lessens the need to shield yourself with hyper-positivity. So if you catch yourself being hyper-positive, give yourself a break. Trust that with awareness, you can balance genuine positivity with your truth. And in this balance, you will find authenticity.

Dismantling the Lies We Tell Ourselves

The excuses—or outright lies—we tell ourselves are how we rationalize our own behavior or the behavior of others to avoid establishing boundaries. It is also a form of resistance to justify not having a difficult conversation or calling out bullshit.

We don't lie to ourselves consciously, of course, but rationalizations and excuses that are not based in fact can be powerful blocks to being known and speaking our truth. You might think, *It's just easier for me to do things myself*, instead of asking your significant other to help more with household chores. That strategy might work to avert the confrontation, but lingering feelings of resentment will remain.

Do you find yourself making excuses for other people's less-than-awesome behavior? It could sound like, "He's under so much pressure at work right now, I know that's why he screamed at me last night." Or, "I know she doesn't mean it when she says hurtful things to me. She is just going through a rough time right now."

This behavior can also be fueled by fear of retaliation. We nullify our own experience, telling ourselves, *I'm afraid I'm making a big deal out of nothing*. Or we talk ourselves out of speaking up because we fear being seen in a negative light, such as, *If I go to human resources, I might be labeled as a drama queen or a troublemaker*. This self-abandoning behavior is *not* the same as consciously choosing our battles. Telling ourselves lies is a way of avoiding having agency over our lives and our experiences and to minimize conflict or confrontation.

TRUE TALK *Rationalizing and making excuses impedes our ability to speak truthfully and establish healthy boundaries.*

BACK TO YOU:
Do You Excuse Bad Behavior?

Take a moment now to think about the questions below to help identify where you might be making excuses for the crap behavior of others.

- Are you *too* understanding of other people's unacceptable behavior? Especially if you know that they are going through a rough time or had a difficult childhood? (Shout-out to the empaths and highly sensitive folks here.)

- Do you preemptively supply excuses for bad behavior to avoid confrontation?

- Do you accept lame excuses from the offenders themselves, essentially letting them (and you) off the hook? Basically, they are not required to take responsibility for their behavior, and you get to avoid asserting yourself—a win-win for perpetuating emotional dysfunction.

If you answered yes to any of these questions, the odds are good that you're ready to kick this behavior to the curb. Please, take a moment to celebrate your desire to change, instead of dwelling on what you were not able to do until now. As Louise Hay said, "The point of power is always in the present moment."

Connecting the Dots

We've covered a good deal of critical material in this chapter. You may have experienced some overwhelm in exploring how your Boundary Blueprint is connected to present-day boundary missteps. That is totally normal. Take a big breath and exhale. You are not alone.

Time and time again, I have heard clients express a profound sense of calm when they see, at last, that they can craft a more appropriate and empowering Boundary Blueprint for themselves. What a relief to know that our ingrained, habitual behaviors can be transformed to conscious choices.

That is exactly how Rachel felt when she completed unpacking her Boundary Blueprint and began to truly examine how her outdated boundary paradigm was showing up in her life, especially in her relationship. In some moments, she felt bowled over by the amount of boundary dysfunction she'd inherited from her family. But she also knew that it was her life to figure out now, and she was committed to changing. It wasn't like she followed a checklist and then one day woke up with an all-encompassing understanding. Like most of my clients, her process was like shedding layers of comfortable and even beloved clothing that no longer fit her. Her break-free moment came when she finally rejected the biggest lies she'd been telling herself: namely, that she needed to achieve a certain amount of financial security before being ready (and worthy) for a fulfilling, reciprocal relationship, and that her boyfriend's less-than-respectful behavior worked for her. I mean, on a subconscious level his bad behavior did work for her. (Hello, secondary gain!) But on a more authentic and freeing level, not at all.

With courage, she named her true feelings and got herself out of the unhealthy pattern of accepting what was actually unacceptable to her. This is so important. When you can do that in your own life, you will stop colluding with the other person's **lowest** instincts and behavior.

Eventually, Rachel ended her relationship and embraced **the** pain that followed. That pain was the path to her liberation. **Over** time, she built the skills to speak up truthfully in the moment **and** draw effective boundaries in her relationships. She eventually **fell in** love with a creative director and for the first time in her life felt **seen** and loved for who she was. As daunting as it might seem to do **your** own deep dive into the basement of your psyche, that same **libera-** tion can be yours, too.

By examining everything we explored in this chapter, you **will** regain loads of time and energy to focus on yourself rather **than** obsessing on the behavior of others. Staying stuck in dysfunctional patterns zaps your life force. That fact alone will hopefully give **you** the motivation needed to unpack the crap out of the unconscious beliefs that are currently directing your behavior.

Refuel your tank with a walk in nature or a cup of your **favorite** tea. Once you feel ready, we're off to learn about Repeating **Boundary** Patterns. Woooo-hoooooo!

▶ BOUNDARY BOSS IN ACTION ◀

1. **Top of Mind.** Sneaky Boundary Blocks crop up in your daily life *all the time.* So pay attention. Are you doing the Insta-Yes? Over-giving? Refusing help? Making excuses for bad behavior? Keep these patterns top of mind, and you will become more aware of how your unique Boundary Blocks are being expressed in your relationships.

2. **Go Deeper: Boundary Blueprint, Big Picture Edition.** You will need some time to fully unpack your Boundary Blueprint, but this is one of *the* cornerstones of your Boundary Boss journey. Don't skip it! Make a self-love date in your calendar, snuggle up in your Zen Den, and go to page 242 in the "Go Deeper" section at the back of the book to get the necessary guidance for this important work.

CHAPTER 5

Digging Deeper
Now Is Not Then

ASHLEY, A TOUGH AND WICKEDLY funny trauma nurse, was suffering from night sweats, insomnia, and "hating everyone" courtesy of menopause, when she initially came to see me for stress reduction and sleep-aid techniques. After only a few sessions, she declared that she was done with dating because her "picker was broken" and fessed up to pretty much a lifetime of dysfunctional and abusive relationships. In the next breath, she mentioned that when she was two months old, her father had abandoned her, her mother, and her brother. It was not exactly *He went out for a pack of smokes and never came back*, but close.

According to her mother, her father claimed to have secured a "great job" in another state and promised to send for the family as soon as he found a place for them to live. They never heard from him again—like, not a peep. Instinctively, I knew that there was a link between this traumatic event, her current stressed-out condition, and her history of boundary-challenged relationships.

Then, a few months into treatment, as we were unpacking Ashley's Boundary Blueprint, she casually told me that *she* was the reason her father left, as if stating an indisputable truth. *The sky is blue, and as a newborn, I caused my family's breakup.*

"Why do you think that?" I inquired.

Ashley shrugged and said, "Well, that's what my mother said."

If Ashley's mother had said that just once, that alone could have left a scar. But her mother repeated that painful story throughout Ashley's entire life, essentially blaming Ashley for the family rupture pretty much any chance she got. Her older brother agreed and often reinforced this narrative. That Ashley's birth caused her father's abandonment was simply family lore, one of those accepted, unquestioned faux facts. When I asked how an infant could be responsible for the actions of an adult, she looked genuinely perplexed. "Huh," she said, "Never thought about it."

This was one of Ashley's greatest limiting beliefs.

Limiting Beliefs

Limiting beliefs, like Ashley's, are seeded in childhood, and yet we may have no idea that they exist or how they impact our behavior and identity. In my experience, when they unconsciously become a part of our identity, deep intimacy is out of reach. Limiting beliefs prevent us from accurately knowing ourselves, which makes being authentically known by others impossible. And we all deserve to be authentically known.

In the last chapter, we examined how unknown material inherited from our family and culture drives exasperating, confusing, and deeply unsatisfying relationships, situations, and boundaries. Now it's time to whip out the rubber gloves cuz we've got some more clearing out to do in the basement. This time around we're going to work on a more granular level, acknowledging how *specific* limiting beliefs become embedded in our blueprint and pave the way for painful (unconscious) repetitions of childhood experiences in our adult lives.

This next-level psychological detox requires bravery, curiosity, designated time in your Zen Den, an open mind—and even a little vigilance. As I like to say, you can't get the healthy bod of your dreams by going to the gym once (much as we might wish otherwise).

Similarly, with a whole lot of crap in our basement, we must stay committed to revealing what has been repressed or gone unexamined.

Ashley, with her over-achieving work ethic, was up for the job. She had been indoctrinated to believe that she single-handedly destroyed her family and her mother's life. That lie set the stage for the rest of Ashley's life. In this light, her habits of working beyond reasonable limits, gravitating toward unhealthy, toxic romantic relationships, and living in a state of hyper-vigilance made sense, as she felt unworthy. Even *questioning* this taken-for-granted tale was a revelation for Ashley. She was waking up to the ways in which she had been participating in her own imprisonment. Her jailbreak needed to start with unearthing how this limiting belief had shaped her behavior, choices, and identity.

Limiting beliefs or childhood stories don't originate only from what parents, teachers, caregivers, and society say about us. Often, children will construct a narrative to try to make sense of difficult circumstances. This is common.

Here's an example: For years, I unwittingly carried a belief that I was a disappointment to my father because I was his last shot at having a son. When this limiting belief came into my awareness, I realized that much of my adult ambition had been driven by a hidden compulsion to prove myself worthy—not exactly a choice. Since my father had already passed away, I asked my mother, a straight shooter, what she thought. According to her, my father was not disappointed by having daughters and did not long for a son. That was fascinating to me. As a child, I had created my own limiting story about my father's feelings to soften the blow of my actual experience. It was waaaaay less painful to think my gender was the problem than to accept that my father simply had no real interest in me. Many children write their own stories to fill in the blanks like I did when they can't make sense of unpleasant or even traumatic experiences.

BACK TO YOU:
What's Your Racket?

Let's begin dismantling your unique limiting beliefs right now. Take a moment to think about your "racket," the story you have about your worth, your capabilities, or your potential that might be hindering your ability to create healthy boundaries in your relationships.

Check out this list of limiting beliefs I've witnessed over the past two decades:

- I'm bad with numbers.

- I'm too sensitive.

- I always pick the wrong partner (just like my mother).

- I'm unlucky in love.

- I made bad choices so I deserve what I get.

- I can't trust myself.

- I'm too broken to be fixed.

- It's my job to make sure everyone else is okay. This is life.

Do any of these ring a bell? If not, take a few moments to identify your racket. Write it down.

When you are aware of the stories that negatively impact the full expression of yourself, you can question why you have that belief and decide to release it. You can then consciously choose to focus on what's right about you and your life, learn to speak to your strengths and achievements, and accept recognition with grace and gratitude.

TRUE TALK *Limiting beliefs are seeded in childhood and can negatively impact our boundary behaviors and self-identity.*

When our limiting beliefs (self-made or inherited) go undiscovered, we hold those limiting beliefs as truth. These so-called truths work to our detriment long after their usefulness has expired. They have the potential to negatively impact our self-esteem, level of worthiness, quality of life, and relationships. This was the case for Ashley. This was the case for me. And it might just be the case for you, too.

As you continue to percolate on what your limiting beliefs might be, let's get clear about what constitutes the "truth" in these situations. When it comes to human interactions and feelings, no one has cornered the market on *the* truth. In Don Miguel Ruiz's wildly popular book *The Four Agreements*, which is based on ancient Toltec wisdom, the second agreement is, "Don't take anything personally." Ruiz believes that we are deeply entrenched in our own subjective reality, so what others say about us reveals more about them than us.

As children, we do not have this complex insight. So these false notions get planted, and without intervention, they keep growing. According to psychologist Carl Rogers, caregivers or parents teach children *conditions of worth*, the standards of behavior that children must follow to receive love and avoid criticism. So, as a child, if your parents said, "You're valuable," you believed it. If they said, "You're worthless," you believed that, too.

Developing little humans don't have the choice to reject unfair treatment or question a suspect narrative from the people they depend on for survival. Children are the ultimate captive audience. Trolling Craigslist for a room-share situation when we're, say, seven years old isn't an option. Our parents or caregivers have total control. When they are unaware of their own dysfunctional imprinting, they may implicitly, or explicitly, convey damaging messages to us, their children.

Ashley's mother was in a state of extreme distress as a young, suddenly single parent with two small children to care for. Most likely, she needed someone to blame for her life blowing up. Ashley, from the time she was an infant, was a convenient target for her mother's pain, rage, humiliation, and disappointment. When Ashley was a child, it wouldn't have occurred to her to question what her mother, her sole caregiver, told her. She counted on her mom for basic survival, as all children do.

It is vitally important to reveal and understand the subjective nature of your childhood "truths" because it is this understanding that will open wide the possibility for better, more expansive stories and/or beliefs about yourself.

We continued to process Ashley's feelings about being scapegoated. (Talk about involuntarily taking one for the team—sheesh.) She began to get in touch with feelings of anger, sadness, and loss that had been securely tucked away in her unconscious. Together, we established that an infant who did not choose to be born cannot be held responsible for the family split. We focused on honoring and healing Ashley's childhood wounds by continuing to deconstruct her limiting self-beliefs and mourning the childhood she never had.

Your Truth and Nothing But
Ashley's unconscious belief that her mere existence was bad enough to inspire her father to permanently leave her entire family made her feel unworthy, guilty, and full of shame. Those feelings led her to unhappy and destructive situations in her personal and professional life. Her chosen field, emergency medicine, meant that daily doses of chaos and intensity were a given for Ashley. She had chosen to work almost double the amount of time required, in one of Manhattan's busiest Level 1 trauma centers, no less. Three 12-hour shifts a week was the norm, with the option for overtime. Ashley usually worked five to six days a week at that pace. This was no accident.

Being immersed in life-and-death situations was a powerful distraction from self-reflection. There was also a powerful element of self-abandonment at play: how little Ashley considered her own mental and physical health. Situations like gunshot wounds, car accident victims, and traumatic brain injuries always took precedence over her own needs. Her job was a perfect fit, really. It was almost like she was unconsciously doing time for a crime she *believed* she'd committed.

That guilt and shame informed all of her decisions—and relationships. She unconsciously colluded with the abusers she inevitably fell for. Down deep, a part of her believed she deserved it. Menopause had tipped the scale. If she could not sleep, there was only so long that she could keep up that grueling pace, which is the only reason she ended up on my couch. That's where she began to realize that no amount of self-punishment or over-functioning could change her mother's perception of events—or her mother's perception of her.

TRUE TALK *Revealing and understanding the subjective nature of your limiting childhood "truth" opens up the possibility for better, more expansive stories or beliefs about yourself.*

Repeating Boundary Patterns

We've established that Ashley's limiting beliefs greatly damaged her self-worth, but there's more to her disordered boundary story. In both Ashley's romantic relationships and her unrelenting devotion to her patients were also Repeating Boundary Patterns in which she unconsciously recreated situations from her early childhood (read: her abandoning father and abusive mother) in her present-day life. As an adult, she unwittingly continued to seek out relationships and lifestyles that echoed her early life experience, even though that's not at all what she wanted consciously.

Maybe you can relate. Have you ever felt like you keep repeating the same *wrong* relationship over and over? This might manifest as repeatedly dating the same unavailable/overbearing/irresponsible/underemployed/controlling (insert your own crappy adjective here) person. Or you might regularly end up with a boss who's a jerk or a narcissist. Or you might continue to be rejected or betrayed by close pals. You get the picture.

These frustrating situations are your Repeating Boundary Patterns. You may consciously swear you will *not* end up doing all the work in your relationship like your mother did, or in a bickering marriage similar to your folks' marriage, but lo and behold—there you are, recycling the same teeth-gnashing feelings you've pretty much spent your entire life attempting to avoid.

It can be confounding and more than a little depressing to find yourself replaying the same unsatisfying interactions, leading to the same undesirable outcomes. Trust me, you are not alone, my dear. Or crazy. Or bad at life. An unconscious compulsion to repeat undesirable experiences is common, *and* there's a major upshot: with information, effort, and guidance, this compulsion is 100 percent curable.

Shout-out to our folks or the caregivers who raised us: we repeat the good stuff they taught and showed us, in addition to repeating the dysfunction. It can be hard to acknowledge both realities, the good and the bad, at once. In fact, for many of us with caregiving tendencies, we feel an obligation to make our parents (and their parenting) okay, even when that comes at the expense of our own well-being. Some find that acknowledging the negative experiences and feelings gives them emotional freedom, as they are then able to appreciate what was positive and endearing with more sincerity. If at any point you start to feel bad, guilty, or ungrateful, just stop, snuggle up in your Zen Den, breathe, light a candle, and journal about how you're feeling. And remember that your experiences are valid. *You have a right to the way you feel.*

Not only that, but it's vital that you feel it. If you grew up in a very enmeshed family system that demanded "group think" (meaning, it discouraged independent thought), your early education taught you to bury your authentic feelings and responses if they differed from that of the group.

Your healing can only come from honoring your experiences and real feelings. The adult in you has probably been rationalizing and making excuses for why your folks failed you the way they did. (I don't need to know them to *know* they did cuz they're flawed humans just like the rest of us.) This is the moment to prioritize your actual truth. Let's agree right now that all of our people did the best they could with the consciousness they possessed at the time. If they could have done it better, we will be generous and assume they would have.

The point of going back to your childhood experiences is *not* to condemn anyone, but to understand. You also need to be willing to separate your image of your parents now (if they are still living) from who they were then. For example, you might have a parent who got sober ten years ago. Yay, parent! The instinct may be to look at their accomplishment and celebrate that, while pushing aside your lived experience as a helpless child of an alcoholic. But you know who doesn't give a shit about that ten-year AA chip? Twelve-year-old you, who might have found them sleeping in the still-running car in the driveway at 5 a.m. and felt like the well-being of your entire family now rested on your child shoulders. *That* kid needs our compassion and care.

TRUE TALK *When Repeating Boundary Patterns are active, it's as if the child within each of us is desperately seeking a do-over of a disappointing, painful, or traumatizing childhood experience to create a better outcome. Without new skills or knowledge, a better outcome is unlikely.*

Do you have a childhood experience that is still charged in your psyche? Part of the reason it's still charged is because it has gone unexamined and is therefore still fueling your behavior in some way. See what I mean? You may also find that you are carrying resentment, which is also vital to acknowledge and release. A requirement of the Boundary Boss process is to honor *all* of our experiences, because for once in your life this is actually just about *you*.

Déjà Vu, All Over Again

The concept of Repeating Boundary Patterns was inspired by Freud's theory of *repetition compulsion*, which he described as, "The desire to return to an earlier state of things." This is based on the idea that humans seek comfort in the familiar, even if it's painful. It's human nature to repeat experiences, whether positive, benign, or outright destructive.

In my therapy office, I have seen the unconscious compulsion to recreate dysfunctional boundary patterns time and time again. A woman who, as a child, was scared of her rigid, perfectionistic mother may find herself in relationships with controlling people she can never please. A woman who was sexually violated by her uncle may gravitate toward relationships with men who disrespect her, thereby confirming her belief that there's something inherently wrong with her. As a therapist, I use the current, repeating issues of my clients as a map to locate the original injuries that need our attention so that they may be released from destructive boundary patterns.

From the standpoint of the conscious mind, this phenomenon of recreating past experiences may seem counterintuitive. *How could the comfort of a painful, but familiar, situation be superior to an unknown situation?* But from the standpoint of the unconscious mind, repetition compulsion makes stunning sense. It is our mind's way of hoping for a better outcome. When Repeating Boundary Patterns are active, the child within each of us is desperately seeking a do-over of a disappointing, painful, or traumatizing childhood experience. Even though the form of repetition may be destructive and harmful, there is a seed of self-healing love contained within the impulse.

Have you ever been in a bad relationship and thought, *This time it's going to be different*? With no evidence or reason to think this, apart from your desire for it to be so? Humans can be a hopeful bunch, but real talk here—without awareness of toxic material that might be lurking in your basement, it's unlikely that you'll have a clear understanding of where in childhood the bad boundary pattern originated. And without that understanding, it's highly unlikely that you will develop the skills to create a better outcome. Luckily, identifying what you might be repeating and why is exactly what we are hitting next.

The 3Qs for Clarity

Ready for some more happy news? Figuring out how your past is interfering with present-day situations and relationships is actually a relatively straightforward process. We simply follow the thread of our feelings to connect the dots from present-day conflict to historical injury. Yes, love, it's quite possible that undesirable feelings you have today are rooted in old feelings that were either unacknowledged or unprocessed. The way we scope them out is by asking three simple questions, the 3Qs for Clarity, which I'll explain in a moment.

To illustrate, I'll share the story of my client Sandy, a 28-year-old paralegal who was experiencing increasingly heated conflict at work with a coworker she described as a "real bully." Pushed to the brink, Sandy had been ruminating over this situation and losing sleep for weeks. She was scared of lashing out and losing her job as a result.

In unpacking Sandy's professional history, a pattern began to emerge. In her last few jobs, she always had a female archenemy who took up plenty of her energetic and emotional bandwidth.

The fact that she'd had this experience, not once, not twice, but three times was significant. I sensed she was unconsciously recreating an outdated dynamic. When I asked her what she thought about this repeating pattern, she said, "Come on, Terri! I'm sure this type of thing happens to everyone."

Actually, nope. It does not.

First, I asked her if any of the archenemies reminded her of anyone. She bit her lip and said, "I don't know." (First Q: Who does this person remind me of?)

Then, I asked if she could identify where in her life she'd felt this way before. (Second Q: Where have I felt like this before?)

And, finally, what was familiar about the way she interacted with these archenemies? How was the behavioral dynamic familiar to her? (Third Q: How is this behavioral dynamic familiar to me?)

That last question sparked an *aha* moment.

"Oh. My. Gosh," she replied. "All three of them are like my sister, Liz. I don't mean they look like her, but they remind me of her, each in their own annoying way. A bossy bully who trampled over me to get what she wanted."

Voila! By going through the 3Qs, we traced Sandy's past relationships to find the unconscious root of her current situation.

What Sandy was experiencing can be described, in psychotherapeutic terms, as a *transference*. When you're experiencing a transference, you are being unconsciously triggered by a person or a situation, and your heightened reaction is fueled by an earlier unresolved experience that is similar to the current situation or person. This is not to say that what Sandy experienced in real time was a figment of her imagination. Rather, her reaction to these controlling or entitled women (in her opinion) was amplified by her unresolved feeling about painful childhood conflicts with her sister, Liz. It's like unconsciously seeking a do-over but with the wrong people.

For example, a Broadway producer casting for roles may be turned off by a brilliant actress for no other reason than the fact that she reminds him of his horrible ex-wife. Or your authoritarian boss reminds you of your punitive parent, so that whenever they're around, you cower. Your present response is being fueled by unresolved pain or feelings from a previous injury. It's like unknowingly hopping into an emotional time machine. Can you see how this would compromise and complicate the crap out of decision-making, effective communication, and your ability to establish and maintain healthy boundaries?

TRUE TALK *Your healing can only come from honoring your real experiences and feelings.*

Now that we understood the origin of Sandy's transference reactions, we knew where to focus our time and energy in her sessions: processing and deactivating her childhood injuries from interactions with her domineering sister. Once that process was complete, Sandy had no more work foes. I'm not kidding. Sandy literally stopped talking about what a bully Betty from work was after only three sessions of unpacking her basement boxes labeled "Lizzy, Original Archenemy." Betty was the same, but Sandy had changed. By talking out and honoring her repressed, painful experiences with her sister, she no longer needed to act it out, using Betty as the surrogate. This simple, straightforward process can work just as effectively for you, too.

Connecting the dots between current challenges and unresolved conflicts or injuries from the past can help you make more informed choices and decisions. It's all about following your feelings. How you feel in a current repeating conflict is likely an echo of how you felt in an early childhood injury. When experiencing a transference, you are caught in the throes of old, charged reactions. The goal is to create enough understanding and internal space so you can mindfully respond, instead of instinctually react, making boundary decisions consciously in the here and now.

BACK TO YOU:
How to Use the 3Qs

The 3Qs tool is a tried-and-true strategy to quickly uncover when the past is negatively impacting the present. It is super simple. Try it now so you will have it when you need it later. Bring to mind a conflict that seems like a repetition or a familiar, unsatisfying situation and ask yourself:

1. Who does this person or situation remind me of?

2. Where have I felt like this before?

3. How is this behavioral or situational dynamic familiar to me?

Once you've asked the 3Qs, you can dig deeper into the transference by asking: When I am in conflict, feeling let down, or having issues in a relationship, who do I become (symbolically), and who do they become?

For example, you may feel like you turn into your ten-year-old self, and your boss may represent your punitive parent. This can further heighten your awareness of the past wounds you are unconsciously carrying (and repeating) and expand your opportunity for healing.

Seeing Is Healing

As a result of her new clarity, for the first time in her adult life, Ashley stopped working overtime. (Three 12-hour shifts a week instead of five felt like "a vacation," she said.) She gradually released her limiting beliefs, learning how to diffuse her historically fueled reactions and behavioral patterns. This process opened up space for her to consciously explore real self-care and build real self-worth. She started sleeping more than five hours a night, doing yoga, eating better, and enjoying a pottery class that she described as cathartic and therapeutic.

Deconstructing, questioning, and eventually rejecting her limiting beliefs profoundly changed her self-image, too. She began to experience herself as someone worthy of care. We also handled her menopause symptoms without drugs. Besides our weekly appointment, Ashley developed a dedicated daily meditation practice and saw an energy coach once a week long after her presenting problems were under control. It turned out that prevention and maintenance were where it was at for Ashley. And probably for you, too.

Decades later, I still have the little lopsided bud vase that Ashley made for me in her first pottery class (which did not actually hold water, lol). To me, the vase is a reminder of the genuine transformation that comes from delving into unconscious beliefs. It's a tangible testament to a powerful truth, that relief from suffering and sustainable change *is* possible.

TRUE TALK *Clearing out the basement (your unconscious mind) of corrupted data and limiting beliefs gives you more space to plant the seeds of positive and productive thoughts and behaviors.*

Over time, you will become crystal clear about the choices you have at your disposal. As a child you didn't have a choice, but luckily for all of us, now is *not* then. *Hallelujah!*

As a grown-up with increased awareness, you have choices about what you think, how you feel, what your truth is, and what it can be. This might just turn out to be one of the most liberating and mind-blowing realizations of your entire life. Clearing out your basement gives you more space to plant the seeds of positive and productive thoughts and behaviors, and before you know it, your new normal is one you consciously designed. You can now take off those protective gloves and throw yourself a little dance party. (Cue the tunes and toss the confetti!)

Stop right now to acknowledge how far you have come in these first five chapters, and take a moment to celebrate! You have familiarized yourself with healthy boundaries, codependency, effective and ineffective communication, your boundary inheritance, your limiting beliefs, and how to get unstuck. That's a lot. Your consciousness has expanded, and that's an enormous achievement. From here on out, the Boundary Boss journey will be focused on how you can use your heightened awareness to enact real-life change and have more personal agency over your amazing, one-of-a-kind life.

▶ BOUNDARY BOSS IN ACTION ◀

1. **Top of Mind.** Pay attention to when you feel quickly or extremely hurt, angry, afraid, or annoyed during an interaction, or right afterward. Use these moments as opportunities to use the 3Qs to uncover potential transference reactions.

2. **Go Deeper: The Resentment Inventory.** Revealing and honoring the resentments you're carrying is a valuable part of your healing process. Go to page 244 in the "Go Deeper" section at the back of the book to access a simple yet powerful exercise to release resentment.

PART 2

Creating the New Normal

CHAPTER 6

The 3Rs

Recognize-Release-Respond

"I CAN'T TAKE IT ANYMORE," Magdalena exclaimed as she threw herself down on my couch for her Friday session. Magdalena was a thirty-something financial advisor who was extremely competent. She rarely got worked up about her job, so I had a feeling that her current exasperation wasn't about her professional life. Magdalena had a voluptuous figure that often drew comments and stares from men on the street—a frequent topic in our therapy sessions.

"What happened?" I asked.

Sighing, Magdalena told me that she was walking down the street when she passed a construction site and heard the old familiar catcalls. "Oooooh, girrrl! Keep strutting them happy hips."

"Terri," she said, shaking her head, clearly agitated. "I wasn't *strutting* anything. I was late for an appointment. I was hurrying down the street. Why can't I just go about my day like a normal person and not draw this kind of attention?"

"What was it about this time that feels different to you? Why can't you 'take it anymore'?" I inquired.

"I don't know. Something inside me just snapped," she replied.

Magdalena went on to explain that the unwanted attention prompted her to run into the nearest clothing store and purchase a knee-length "grandma" sweater, even though she only had four blocks to go. This impulse buy loosely covered her figure, but it also made her late for her appointment.

Moments like this happened to Magdalena all the time. Personally, I thought she was gorgeous, but that's not what Magdalena thought, which is what mattered. As a child, she had an older sister who was always thin, and when their cousin's size-2 hand-me-downs came in the mail, Magdalena, a size 12, was always the odd girl out. No one in her family had tried to make her feel bad about her size. Still, it was hard not to notice that her mother, at meals, said things like, "Aren't you full, though?" and kept an eye on how much Magdalena ate. In middle school, Magdalena was teased by her peers for developing breasts early. This began a lifelong pattern of wanting to hide.

When Magdalena had landed in my office, she was firm in her belief that she was "too big." Her poor body image clearly contributed to low self-worth. As a result, these frequent, unwanted interactions on the street reinforced her belief that there was something gravely wrong with her. Her shame ballooned with every new, "Hey, hot stuff!" Long after scurrying by yet another construction site with her head down and a sharp pain in her chest, Magdalena continued to feel terrible.

I didn't blame her for not liking the catcalls. I hoped, though, that she would come to realize that she could choose to relate to these moments differently and, more importantly, choose more affirming thoughts about her intrinsic value and self-image.

"There's *got* to be a better way!" she exclaimed.

For Magdalena and anyone else who has reached a tipping point with frustrating situations, indeed there is a better way. That's not to say we can manage other people's words or actions. Often, we can't. But we can learn to respond differently. And we can definitely learn not to internalize other people's judgments. *Recognize-Release-Respond* is a three-part strategy for learning to *recognize* when we are having a historical or disordered reaction; to *release* any transference and physical symptoms that might be occurring; and to *respond* with mindfulness, based on what we want to create. The 3Rs strategy helps us establish new behavioral norms.

Before we explore how the 3Rs work in greater detail, let's discuss how we're neurologically wired to create new behavioral norms (yes, it's true!), as well as how we can tap into our body wisdom to gain important intel on our boundary behaviors. Body wisdom is an integral piece of recognizing when you're either in the midst of a Repeating Boundary Pattern or about to be swept up in one.

You Can Teach Your Old Brain New Tricks

Changing long-standing behavioral patterns can feel plenty daunting. The previous chapters were designed to help you raise your awareness about the unconscious drivers of your habituated behaviors, but awareness alone is not enough. Altering your behavior once isn't enough, either. You have to change your behavior *repeatedly*. Many of these behavioral patterns have been in place for decades, so it is gonna take a minute to course correct. But getting what you want is worth the work.

There's a good reason to put in the effort to repeatedly make healthier choices. Neuroscience helps to explain why.

Until the late 1960s, brain experts thought that the brain reached full development in childhood and then stayed fixed until old age, when the inevitable decline in cognitive functioning began. Not so, says science today. Five decades ago, brain scientists discovered a game-changing truth: the brain is changeable and adaptable. You *can* teach an old brain new tricks. In fact, the brain's neural connections—estimated to be in the ballpark of a whopping 100 trillion—are formed and potentially altered every single day, thanks to our lived experiences. This is called neuroplasticity.

When we continue with our familiar habits and patterns that leave us feeling upset, dejected, angry, and despairing, all we're doing is staying stuck in our old crap stew. But it truly doesn't have to be that way. With concerted, consistent effort, we can choose to work with our ever-changing brain to become more flexible and creative—increasing our well-being exponentially.

Taking Actions That Make a Difference

Magdalena needed to shift. She could no longer stand to inhabit such a tiny piece of existential real estate in the world, playing small and hating on herself. My guess is that you may have found yourself in a similar pinch.

To harness the power of your brain's plasticity, you first have to *want* to change, and then you need to be willing to back up that desire with new actions.

Meditation

In my twenties, my therapist suggested I learn to meditate, explaining the neurological and therapeutic benefits of a dedicated practice. Since I was always looking for a shortcut, I immediately found a weekend intensive, thinking I could just check meditation off my to-do list. Little did I know that there was no shortcut. It took a long time for me to successfully establish a dedicated daily practice.

I turned a corner when I realized that regularly sitting in stillness and silence added about three seconds to my response time. That doesn't sound like much, but those three seconds created the internal space I needed to respond more—and react less. Less drama, more joy. Once I experienced the benefits of meditation firsthand, I became a true believer and certified instructor. I started creating guided meditations for my clients to make this transformative practice as accessible as possible. (Get started with the simple meditation on page 238.)

In a contemplative state, we open ourselves up to heightened awareness of what is not working for us, *and* we create more mental space. Mindfulness allows us to slow down, recognize what's going on, release our old, knee-jerk reactions, and instead respond with more intention.

Tapping into Body Wisdom

Meditation can help you become more aware of your body, too, by allowing you to slow down and realize you're not just your thoughts, nor is your brain the only valuable source of information. In fact, the sparkling wisdom of your body is *always* available and can help you to become aware of when you're not comfortable or when you need to take a different tactic. Trust me, if you pay attention to visceral sensations, you *will* get valuable intel about what you need to do.

Body wisdom, once you tap into it, can become your secret weapon in shifting from dysfunctional boundary patterns to healthier ones. Because it's completely possible to know *intellectually* that you need to do something differently *and also* shy away from taking that new action. Learn to listen to the knots in your stomach. The constriction in your chest. The pain in your throat. The throbbing of your head. These bodily sensations are trying to help you. They are pointing you in a new direction, and they are proof that the body is your compass to the most healing and empowering path.

Here's a real-life story to illustrate this point. My friend Jean, a high-functioning codependent (HFC) and empath, was always coming home drained. It seemed like wherever she was, the neediest person in the room always found her. Not wanting to be rude, she would listen as they unloaded, her stomach in knots, excusing herself once the other person's crap-tastic stream of consciousness had run its course. Sometimes that took an hour—no joke. Because she set no limits, she'd take on way too much and often feel bad for hours and sometimes days afterward.

BACK TO YOU:
Bells + Breathing for Mindfulness

Most of us have been ignoring the signals of our bodies for far too long. To be mindfully dialed in to your body wisdom is to bring your awareness to how you're feeling in the present moment and to have the intention to listen.

Below is a simple mindfulness exercise you can do a few times a day. It's incredibly effective.

1. Set the alarm on your cell phone (a bell is nice—be gentle) to go off every three to four hours. When you hear the alarm, have the intention to pause for 30 to 60 seconds.

2. Use this 30 to 60 seconds to check in with how you're feeling. Close your eyes, breathe deeply, and do a quick scan of your body from head to toe. Every time you reach an area that feels constricted or painful, stop and take a long, slow, deep breath. Notice the sensation there. Then breathe directly into that spot and visualize the unwanted feeling leaving with your exhalation.

3. Next, with your eyes gently closed, ask your body what it needs. Pause and listen for the answer.

The more you listen to and honor the wisdom of your body, the more your intuition will kick in. You will become more and more adept at creating effective internal and external boundaries, too.

A wise pal offered Jean a simple cognitive-behavioral trick. The next time Jean was in one of these draining situations, she put both hands on her stomach, as her friend advised. She reminded herself that she was standing in the line of fire, was choosing to stay there, and that she had options. While it felt incredibly awkward, she did something different this time. She said, "Oh, if you'll excuse me, I need to get going." Jean was so inspired by how effective this new action was that she began regularly employing the hands-on-stomach action. In a matter of weeks, she felt astoundingly better—lighter, freer, and more able to focus on herself. Years later, listening to and honoring her body wisdom has become second nature.

The more you tune in to your body, the clearer your picture of what's not working for you. So often, when we're embroiled in charged situations, it's hard to identify and articulate our true feelings or thoughts. How often have you looked back on a situation and thought in retrospect, *I should have seen the red flags*? Most likely, your body was trying to get your attention, but your attention was dialed out, not in.

I have heard countless stories of persistent bodily sensations sending a deeper message.

One client suspected her live-in boyfriend of cheating. Then she got a mysterious vaginal infection that put a serious damper on their sex life. (Thank you, STD-prevention angels.) Doctors didn't have a clear-cut diagnosis, but they put her on antibiotics. Nothing worked. Her boyfriend joked, "I think you're allergic to me." She laughed, but thought, *Holy crap, he's probably right*. She began to develop a more intimate and loving relationship with her body, which allowed her to get curious about her suspicions. This led to her asking her boyfriend more pointed questions, which resulted in a major *aha* moment. He finally admitted that he'd been having sex with a mutual friend. When she broke up with her boyfriend and moved out, her symptoms cleared up within a week. Thank you, body wisdom! (And bye-bye, bad boyfriend!)

BACK TO YOU:
Learn to Recognize

In order to gain self-knowledge, you must become aware of what interactions activate a stress response. Here are a few questions to ask yourself in the moment to start recognizing what is happening and why:

▫ What am I feeling?

▫ Where in my body am I feeling it?

▫ Did an interaction or thought trigger the feeling?

▫ Am I in the midst of a Repeating Boundary Pattern?

For example, your answers might be:

▫ I feel constricted. I feel dread. I feel uneasy.

▫ It's in my chest, my stomach, my head.

▫ I started feeling constricted after Bob asked me to cover his shift.

▫ After I thought about my interaction with Betty, I started feeling anxious.

What do the 3Qs reveal about my own personal Repeating Boundary Pattern in this moment? How is this interaction familiar to me?

Learning to *recognize* that something feels off during or after interacting with another person is the first step of the 3Rs (Recognize-Release-Respond), which you will learn how to use later in this chapter. With a genuine desire to understand yourself, you are creating internal space for change, and the window of transformation starts to widen.

TRUE TALK *With body wisdom as your guide, you will have an easier time figuring out what is (and what is not) working for you.*

When you don't embrace your body wisdom, you miss out on the opportunity for major mindset shifts. Instead of paying attention, you might resort to taking an Ambien® to fall asleep or having a nightly cocktail, or three, to "wind down." Or flee, numb, or distract yourself in any number of ways. But ignoring your body's messages blocks access to your own growth. You've got to slow down enough to pay attention to the signals.

By moving from judgment to curiosity, you increase your self-knowledge. You become the observer without judgment. If you're stuck in a rut, the occurrences that cause you the most angst are not random. So it would definitely behoove you to stay alert and aware of what might be going on underneath the surface.

With body wisdom as your guide, you will have an easier time figuring out what is (and what is not) working for you. This is *essential* to boundary-setting. The more solid intel you have about your internal reactions and responses (like which interactions cause stress, for example), the better equipped you become to determine what kind of external boundary is most appropriate or what kind of action is needed in a particular situation.

Preferences, Desires, and Deal-Breakers

As you begin to establish boundaries, you will need to understand the difference between your preferences, desires, and deal-breakers. Knowing these distinctions will further clarify what is and isn't okay with you (and to what degree). It will also set you on the path of making decisions that are rooted in your truth.

Preferences. Having a preference means being partial to one option over another. Do you like coffee or tea? Zumba or

SoulCycle? Rising early or sleeping late? These are examples of preferences that are internal and personal. No one else needs to chime in on whether you like a bath over a shower, for example. In our busy lives, many of us never take the time to actually think about our preferences, which is why completing your Okay/Not Okay master list from chapter 2 is an important exercise toward deeper self-knowledge. If you haven't done that yet, now would be a great time to head to page 239 and dive in.

When it comes to the preferences that involve others, however, you are required to communicate. For example, you may like to go to bed early, but your partner might be a night owl. You might say, "I prefer that you come to bed at nine o'clock with me." Your preferences matter, and they're worth talking about. Learning how to express them early and often, with ease and grace, creates the foundation for more satisfaction and harmony in your life. You or your partner might suggest a compromise, like heading to bed early together two nights a week.

Some people will respond to your expressed preference with gratitude for the clarity, such as, "Thank you! I am glad to know that connecting by phone instead of text is important to you." Others, though, will interpret any request as a demand, no matter how carefully you choose your words. That's okay, babe. What matters is that you took action on your own behalf.

Oh, and a word on demands. They do not generally have a place in healthy, mutually reciprocal relationships. You may feel momentarily good making one ("You will come to my mother's house with me or else!"), but ultimately demands smack of entitlement and turn people off. You have choices, and so do the people in your life. Making demands of others kills cooperation and collaboration, which are necessary if you want to get your needs met in a healthy way.

Stating your preference is part of learning to negotiate for your needs. You are opening up a conversation—and a conversation is a two-way street. That means that others may not always agree to it. So often women who begin to (finally!) express their preferences feel dejected when they are met with resistance. When this happens, don't take it as an etched-in-stone referendum on your worth (terrible) or the state of your relationship (doomed). I cannot stress this enough.

Relationships require a give and take. This is why it is so important to make the distinction for yourself about what is simply your preference, what is worth negotiating for, and what is a non-negotiable deal-breaker.

To get your needs met, you have to be willing to be specific about what you would like and then open your mind and heart to a compromise, a conversation, a negotiation, a yes, or a no. Compromising with discernment is important (especially if historically you've been the one who is always giving in). Know the difference between giving in just to keep the peace and making a concession that feels healthy and equitable. If you're always getting the short end of the compromise stick, that's not healthy or equitable.

Being able to receive and respect another person's *no* is as vital to your Boundary Boss status as owning your own *no*. If you're so tender that after hearing a no you decide you'll never ask for anything again, you're not really making room for the other person in your relationship, are you? There can't be only one way for the other person to respond. Yes, it would be great if they agreed with you, but you will find yourself in many instances where that is just not the case. You may need to say something like, "Okay, I hear you. What would you be willing to do, then?" or "What can we do so that we both get our needs met?"

TRUE TALK *To get your needs met, you have to be willing to be specific about what you want and then open your mind and heart to a compromise, a conversation, a negotiation, a yes, or a no.*

Desires. Desires are a step-up from preferences, in that they reveal our most potent wishes. For example, you may have a desire that your partner or best friend understand you emotionally—or at least care enough to try. Hearing that you are "too sensitive" is counter to your closely held wish to be seen, known, and heard. If your desire to be understood continues to go unfulfilled, well, that's most likely going to graduate to a deal-breaker at some point.

As with your preferences and deal-breakers, you define your desires—no one else. Sometimes societal or familial influence clouds our wishes. For example, a friend told me that her youngest daughter was getting married but had no desire for a big, fancy wedding. My friend then pressured her daughter into having "just a small" ceremony. Additionally, she roped her eldest daughter into participating in Operation White Dress, saying to the bride-to-be, "We really think it's the right thing for you to make this commitment in front of your friends and family." Luckily, that bride was crystal clear about not wanting to do any of those things. I secretly rejoiced when I received a postcard from Vegas with a photo of the two self-determined lovers, getting hitched by an Elvis impersonator with "Wish You Were Here" written above their smiling faces.

Sometimes when we are highly sensitive or HFC, we squash our desires when we sense that pursuing (or even expressing) the desire will hurt feelings or provoke a loved one's judgment or wrath. This goes doubly so for empaths. Perhaps when you were a child, you grew accustomed to sensing a parent's non-verbal disapproval. Whatever your experiences, past or present, getting clear on your desires *now* is an act of self-respect.

Deal-Breakers. Deal-breakers are non-negotiable boundaries. Since the external boundaries you create are driven by your internal preferences, deal-breakers are unique to each person. You're the only one who knows what your deal-breakers are, so you need to get comfortable with having a deal-breaker that your loved ones may not understand. For example, I was in a long-term relationship with a man I was compatible with in many ways, except for one big thing. He was sedentary, and I wanted to be with someone who was more active. His couch-potato ways did not match my desire to share a love of fitness *with* my partner. Sure, I could go on hikes with friends or hit the gym solo, but that wasn't the point. I remember telling one friend this, and she said, "But you two seem so happy. Can't you just let this one go?" The truth was that *she* might have been able to let that go, but I knew I couldn't. That deal-breaker led to our breakup. For some, political affiliation can be a deal-breaker, or life vision, such as whether or not to get married, have children, etc.

There are, of course, more dramatic examples of deal-breakers, such as infidelity, betrayal, addiction, or abuse. Especially in these high-stakes situations, knowing your deal-breakers independent of others is crucial. I have seen clients who think that being with an alcoholic or a cheater is nothing they would ever consider until they find themselves emotionally entangled with an alcoholic or a cheater. In these cases, it can be tempting to excuse or rationalize the behavior away. Really, though, your deal-breakers are between you and you. You don't need someone else's validation to make your deal-breaker okay. It's your choice—and more importantly, *your* life.

So get clarity on what's a definite *nope*, and you will have an easier time knowing what to keep and what to discard. To help you know your preferences, desires, and deal-breakers, check out the exercise on page 244.

When we don't speak truthfully, we're living in a vacuum in our own mind. We make assumptions about what's going on for the other person or what they should know about what's going on with us. To express yourself with confidence, let's delve into the 3Rs (Recognize-Release-Respond).

Using the 3Rs

Learning to employ the Recognize-Release-Respond strategy will help you navigate conflict, express yourself with self-assurance, and establish new neural pathways to boot. This is one of the BB strategies that builds the foundation for a life that resonates with your desires.

1. **Recognize.** What's not working for you? How do you feel in your body? Are you reminded of a historical situation, and is that contributing to the sensations in your body? Focus on you and your feelings, instead of judging and making the other person wrong or bad. This is about increasing your self-knowledge and understanding what is good for you—and what's not. Listening to your body can prompt you to get curious about your experience and also to interrupt your normal way of operating, which creates the opening for something better.

2. **Release.** Be brave and willing to step out of your comfort zone. Find and release the physical feeling by breathing deeply into that spot until it expands. Let go of what's familiar, whether a limiting belief or an old

behavioral pattern. Identify any transference, or Repeating Boundary Pattern. Remember that now is not then. Tell yourself, "That's just old stuff," and let it go so that you can be in a more thoughtful and strategic mindset.

3. **Respond.** Choose to speak and act from a more mindful and conscious place. Make a simple request. State your preference, desire, or deal-breaker. Take a new action.

Now that you understand the importance of establishing new behavioral patterns—and how to do it—let's look at how the 3Rs worked for Magdalena and the shame that came up from the unwanted attention she received.

Deep in her unconscious, Magdalena believed she was inherently unworthy. Know that if you have a deep-seated belief, as she did, your unconscious will always be scanning your environment for evidence to support your claims. I like to say that the unconscious mind is the very best executive assistant you've ever had. ("See, boss, you're right; they *are* making fun of you.") To silence that disempowering message, Magdalena first recognized that there was a problem through her body wisdom. This was the beginning of interrupting the unwanted pattern.

Her first clue was the constriction she felt in her chest as she walked down the street. By becoming more mindful through a regular meditation practice, Magdalena started to pay attention to her visceral instincts. As a result, she discovered that she felt anxious *before* hearing anything from men on the street. True, she felt a million times more anxious after, but recognizing that these feelings were present in advance of unpleasant interactions was telling. Energetically she was bracing for the unwanted attention, and that anticipatory energy was playing a significant role in her experiences.

Magdalena started to explore why she didn't love her body and all the thoughts and feelings that accompanied her body shame. Though she was not in relationship with any of the catcalling strangers, her issue was a boundary issue. She felt inhibited walking through the world, which is not the BB way, nor the way I knew she could be. Many people operate under the assumption that boundaries are about keeping unwanted behavior out, which is true to a certain extent. More importantly, though, they protect your sacred space within.

Magdalena couldn't control the catcallers, but she could change her internal dialogue and therefore her experience, to protect herself. As we learned in chapter 5, we always have a hand (conscious or unconscious) in writing our own story. And our internal reality, self-concept, and self-identity are all informed by this story. Magdalena's narrative of being unworthy *was* something she could change.

In my office, Magdalena began to develop genuine acceptance and love for her body. She looked at *all* the ways in which her body allowed her to enjoy her life. She was able to dance salsa, savor her favorite roasted rosemary chicken dish with potatoes *au gratin*, and admire the beauty of nature. None of this would be possible without her body. In becoming more self-loving, Magdalena was able to *release* her negative thoughts and open her mind to having a less charged and more empowering experience. She was starting to understand that her happiness was much more dependent on what *she* thought than on what other people did or didn't do.

In changing her *response*, Magdalena opted to tell a new story. The next time she heard a man say, "Whoa, girl. You look hot!" she smiled and said the same affirmation to herself: *That's right. I do have a fit, fleshy, beautiful bod.* Same butt, same block, same blowhard, but a whole new experience.

The only thing that changed was her mind, allowing her to reach for a more freeing and expansive way of interpreting events. That first experience was super powerful. The new, affirming body story sparked a general sense of enthusiasm, and in time, she began oozing confidence as she walked down the street.

TRUE TALK *Use the 3Rs strategy (Recognize-Release-Respond) to recognize old reactions, release physical symptoms and transferences, and then respond with mindfulness that is aligned with the outcome you desire.*

This shift in perception had a profound domino effect on other areas of her life. She took more initiative at work and decided to put herself out on the dating scene. I could see a tangible shift in how she carried herself even in my office. She sat tall and radiated self-assurance and vibrancy. Finally, Magdalena felt like the goddess she always was, all because she decided to put in the work required to learn a better way of relating to herself.

While Magdalena's boundary issue did not involve loved ones or colleagues, the same principles apply with the people we know and interact with on a more intimate level. For example, a woman whose partner is perpetually committing them both to plans she doesn't like could use the same three-step strategy:

1. *Recognize* how she's actually feeling in the moment, and use this intel as a prompt to interrupt her default reaction. (Silently upset and sick to her stomach.)

2. *Release* any old charge that's based on a past event or limiting story. (*I feel invisible like I did with my father/sister/coach, but I don't have to let my past inform my present.*)

3. *Respond* with a simple request that her partner consult her before purchasing the "Deluxe Super Bowl Travel Package" as a "gift" to celebrate their fifteenth wedding anniversary. (*I love the idea of doing something special together to celebrate our anniversary, and I would like to make a simple request that we decide what that is together.*)

Many of us are prone to assign negative meanings to interactions and experiences we encounter on a daily basis. Those interpretations then dictate our emotional responses and the ways they impact us. Remember, "truth" is subjective. Perspective is where it's *at*.

The In-Between: A Word of Warning (and Encouragement)

Right now, you are at a critical juncture in your Boundary Boss journey. You might be feeling a little raw or even naked, like, *Why did Terri take away all my weapons?* But listen: using indirect, avoidant, or any other ineffective way of communicating may have been a familiar modus operandi in the past, but let's go wide-angle lens here. Although the old ways may be firmly established in the neural pathways of your brain, they have not *actually* been working for you. You know too much to revert to the defense mechanisms and straight-up dysfunctional strategies from the past, but you have not quite mastered the new skill set. I call this phase of personal transformation the *In-Between*.

You went all the way down into the metaphorical basement and flipped on the floodlights. You cannot unsee what you uncovered. That also means you cannot just go back to the old way of being—even if you wanted to. And trust me, you don't.

Typically, the In-Between is a phase where resistance can crop up. Yup, resistance is a game of whack-a-mole until these new behaviors become more fully integrated. That's okay. What's new can also be *very* uncomfortable (hence, resistance!). This is a perfect time to flex those BB muscles. Remember, you are stronger than you think.

TRUE TALK *Taking small, consistent steps to assert yourself will speed up your time in the In-Between. You'll get to the other side of your dysfunctional behavior faster.*

To navigate the In-Between, you might choose to practice your new boundary skills with people lower on your ladder of importance. Naturally, you're invested less in relationships with, say, an acquaintance you only see a couple of times a year or your mail carrier. Instead of feeling a pang of irritation every time you see the previous tenant's mail stuffed in your tiny urban mailbox yet again, and leaving it there with the hope your mail carrier, Phillip, takes the hint, you could make a direct request. "I'd like to bring something to your attention/make a simple request/get this on your radar." (That way, you're less likely to scream, "Sandra Giancarlo hasn't lived here for five years! How do you not know that, Phillip?!") Start with small-stakes, low-impact interactions with low-priority people in your life.

Looking for opportunities to assert yourself is an effective way to shorten the In-Between. Take small steps in the relationships you're more invested in. Tell your partner that you really love spicy buffalo wings, instead of always going along with eating the mild kind that they prefer. (Think about how much more you know about the nitty-gritty preferences of the people in your life than they know about yours.) There are unlimited opportunities for you to start to take up more space in the world, and each time you do, you're reinforcing a vital truth: *you* matter.

Acknowledging your progress step by step creates a well of hope that helps you build resiliency, a much-needed reserve of persistence and dedication. There *will* be hard moments. You *will* want to quit. But please know that there *will* also come a time when your new normal manifests without having to invest so much energy and forethought.

Real talk, lovebug: your comfort zone is a prison. This is the moment to step outside it because that's where everything you truly want exists. We are expanding your perceptions and then following up with new behaviors until that new pattern of being becomes a new neural pathway and your new normal. I'm so excited for you!

▶ BOUNDARY BOSS IN ACTION ◀

1. **Top of Mind.** Pay attention to the cues from your body. Throughout the day, ask yourself, "What do I need right now? Am I hungry, thirsty, tired? Do I need to stretch or move?" Then take the time to give yourself what you need.

2. **Go Deeper: Know Your Preferences, Desires, and Deal-Breakers.** Self-knowledge is one of the foundations you are building your Boundary Boss skill set on. To deepen your self-understanding, go to page 244 in the "Go Deeper" section at the back of the book to drill down on your preferences, desires, and deal-breakers.

3. **Get Inspired: Not Your Mama's Affirmations.** Creating personalized affirmations that resonate with you is a powerful (and fun!) way to inspire transformation. You will find a step-by-step guide on page 245 in the "Go Deeper" section at the back of the book.

CHAPTER 7

From Reactive to Proactive Boundaries

MY CLIENT MARIA ENTERED THERAPY with me because she'd been 50 to 80 pounds overweight her entire adult life, and it had begun to negatively impact her health. She'd tried everything but couldn't seem to successfully lose weight and keep it off. Her efforts, she said, were futile.

"My body hurts. I'm tired. As much as I love my husband, I think he wants me to stay the way I am," she admitted, lowering her head in shame.

I admired her courage. I also had my first glimpse of where our work together would begin.

Married to Gus for twenty years, Maria was a mom-preneur who had stayed home to raise their two children, Cleo and Dimitrious, while she built a successful beauty business, selling vegan skin-care and nutrition products. She described her relationship as happy and mutually supportive. Maria and Gus co-parented well, and both naturally prioritized their children and family life. They enjoyed attending live music shows together and spending quality time with their extended family and friends: summer barbecues, book clubs, and fun, lively dinners. Along with fully participating in their active family and social life, Gus was a patient and attentive listener, Maria reported. It sounded like they had a good thing going.

When I asked her to expand on what was going wrong, she admitted that at the beginning of any weight loss effort, Gus would be encouraging and supportive until about week three or four. (*Kudos for noticing*, I thought.) As soon as a few pounds had come off, she would feel a shift in his attitude and behavior. For example, Gus would bake her favorite crumb cake and tell her that it wouldn't kill her to "treat" herself. Or he would make a reservation for the whole family at their favorite Italian restaurant for a "special occasion."

When we explored further, Maria also shared how instead of being supportive of her attempt to walk twenty minutes a day, Gus would suggest they finish watching something on Netflix or promise to walk with her the next day but then fail to follow through.

Since Gus was normally a supportive partner, I concluded that these sabotaging behaviors likely indicated that he felt unconsciously threatened in some way by the prospect of Maria losing weight.

Our task was to better understand Maria and Gus's current dynamic, including the hidden psychological motivations that had created the situation, and empower Maria to create and communicate healthy boundary requests. That way, she could protect her weight loss goal, initiate conscious communication about it with Gus, and successfully change their boundary dance.

Unspoken Boundary Agreements

From what Maria described, it sounded like she and Gus had silently agreed to avoid conflict, suppress parts of their personalities that might threaten the relationship, and keep each other comfortable. Sound familiar?

Maybe you've had the experience of accepting that a partner or loved one hates direct communication about emotionally charged issues. You tiptoe around problems instead of dealing with them head-on. Another example of an unspoken boundary agreement often shows up in families. Perhaps you have a domineering parent or sibling who attempts to covertly control you with money or unsolicited advice. You don't *like* feeling controlled but instead of saying so, you just nod your head and smile, while burning up with resentment inside.

BACK TO YOU:
Create Clean Agreements

Silent agreements are the unspoken rules of engagement in your relationships. Making assumptions about others is what drives those silent agreements. To see where you might be making assumptions to avoid true talk, take a moment now to ponder the questions below:

- When you really want someone to do something for you, do you ever think they should intuit, understand, or *just know* because to you it's obvious?

- Do you ever allow offensive comments to pass by, telling yourself the other person didn't mean anything by it?

- Do you assume that if you make a big fuss over a pal's birthday that when yours rolls around they will do the same for you?

- Do you ever think, *I shouldn't have to tell her that*, or *He should know that by now?*

Identifying where your assumptions are impacting your ability to communicate clearly is the first step to creating clean, transparent BB-style agreements.

Like our Boundary Blueprints, these silent agreements often go unexamined. Kept in the shadows, they can be mighty destructive. When unspoken boundary agreements are active, you may not feel that speaking up is an option. By now, you are aware, though, that you *always* have options.

Maria had no idea that an unspoken boundary agreement in her marriage was the issue. It seemed clear to me that they both had fears of changing their well-established boundary dance, especially since the overall state of their relationship was positive. For all human beings, this fear of change is often our first hurdle in taking action to establish Proactive Boundary Plans.

Yet the only thing we can count on is change. According to my pal, meditation and mindfulness expert Davidji, change is like breath. It isn't part of the process; it *is* the process. There can be something profoundly liberating about surrendering to the ebbs and flows of life's changes. Making a conscious choice to cozy up to the unknown is *truly* a game changer. You can learn to embrace the unknown, which is where all the infinite possibilities of your life reside.

For many of us, understanding this concept in theory is one thing, but finding tranquility in the midst of change, especially in the context of establishing personal boundaries, is another.

Humans are hardwired to fear change, as we discussed in chapter 3. Even though we no longer find ourselves in the life-threatening situations our ancestors did, fear still comes up. When that bone-deep, primal fear gets hold of us, it's hard to shake free. Fortunately, though, you now have the 3Rs (Recognize-Release-Respond) in your Boundary Boss tool kit to help you press pause on any default physiological reactions. This enables you to respond with more thought and care to any range of anxiety-provoking situations.

You will definitely need to keep those 3Rs in your back pocket. As you progress in your skill building and knowledge of personal boundaries, you may once again encounter some blocks. Maybe you have a fear of success (getting healthier will cause you to lose some of the comforts of your less-than-healthy familiar ways) or a fear of failure (getting healthier might mean risking rejection, discomfort, and imperfection more than before).

> **TRUE TALK** *Be aware that when we fear change, we tend to hold tight to old, familiar behaviors, even when they are not aligned with achieving our desired outcomes.*

Fear of success and fear of failure are two sides of the same coin, and that coin is fear of change. As you peel the onion of your angst and work through its layers, know that fear of change is actually a fear of loss. We lose the familiar to enter the unknown. But with a mindset shift, we can experience change as more exhilarating than terrifying.

Not surprisingly, in established relationships, initiating changes can feel super threatening to both parties, even when we know in our hearts that change must happen.

To help you navigate any fears that may come up around changing established boundary dances, I'm walking you through the nitty-gritty steps of moving from a reactive to proactive boundary strategy. Once you understand *how* to do this, fear might still be there, but it will not stop you from stepping up and speaking your truth.

This step-by-step process prepares you to catch boundary conflicts early, transform any indirect communication habits, and assert yourself with confidence. To be successful, you must identify your preferences, desires, and deal-breakers, as we did in the last chapter, and know (or anticipate) who you're dealing with. You also need to give some thought to what kinds of relationships you want to curate in all areas of your life.

Let's say Bob from your office keeps video-calling you at home, and you don't like it. If you're being boundary-reactive, you may drop some hints by speaking tersely and shooting him some shade (cue the eye-rolling). You hope he'll see you're visibly annoyed and stop. He doesn't, though, and this dance gets old, real quick.

You need to manage Bob instead of hoping he will take a hint, and developing a proactive plan will help. Since new actions and reactions are commonly met with resistance, you can bet that Bob won't like you setting a "work only" parameter. Hey, it makes sense. More importantly, though, your anticipation of discomfort in making any changes is an indicator that you and Bob have an unspoken boundary agreement. By not directly saying, "Cut the shit, Bob," you are essentially agreeing to abide by his invasive boundary behavior.

Proactive Boundary Plans and transparent agreements are vital in any relationship, including those between coworkers, entrepreneurs with their clients, and business partners. They establish your expectations, help you avoid conflict down the line, and increase the chances of having healthy, productive relationships. This is true for other relationships, too, from friendships, to family connections, to neighbors—pretty much everyone. Proactive boundaries set you up for success.

Here's the catch. Whatever relationship you're struggling with now, the onus falls on you to face your fears of making changes to any unspoken agreements. It's up to you to craft your Proactive Boundary Plan. To do that, you first have to check in on your *internal boundaries*, which directly reflect the health of your relationship with yourself.

Internal Boundaries

If boundaries with others are your external boundaries that tell people how you will (or won't) interact with them, *internal boundaries* dictate how you interact with yourself.

Before Maria could establish her Proactive Boundary Plan with Gus, we needed to get clear on her internal boundaries, the experiences and feelings she was allowing within herself. I sensed that her internal boundaries could be healthier. Otherwise, she'd have an easier time turning down that damn crumb cake with a breezy, "None for me, thanks, hon."

Having strong internal boundaries requires self-knowledge and the strength to follow through on your word to yourself (which is why the Okay/Not Okay exercise came early, in chapter 2; flip back and do it now if you skipped it then). For example, you may say that you're going to adopt a new healthy habit of going to yoga every week, but then after a few weeks, you skip class because you're distracted by social media/friends/your couch.

TRUE TALK *Internal boundaries are based on authentic self-knowledge. They dictate the limits you place on experiences and feelings you allow within yourself. They directly reflect the health of your relationship with yourself.*

Hey, you're a human being. You don't have to be perfect, but understand that when you make a promise to yourself and don't follow through (or are otherwise unable to postpone insta-gratification for your own personal betterment), you've abandoned yourself.

Self-abandonment is one of the main symptoms of damaged internal boundaries. Your ability to make healthy choices is compromised. If you abandon yourself consistently, you will always be three steps shy of reaching the finish line of your goals.

Healthy internal boundaries are incredibly valuable. When you have them, you can consistently rely on yourself to do what you say you're going to do. You feel peaceful inside because you trust yourself enough to take care of you. For example, so you can keep your yoga class commitment, ask your mother to show up for your visit an hour later than she'd like. There are two types of boundaries in action here: the internal boundary of keeping your commitment to yourself by not skipping your class, and the external boundary of requesting your mother come an hour later. Or saying no to a *friends with benefits* situation with your ex, when you want a more substantive relationship. You have the clarity of mind to say "not for me" to things that really *aren't* for you because they are counter to your desired outcomes. You value your actual feelings more than your concern about how others will respond to any limits you set. Healthy internal boundaries give you the strength to take actions and make decisions that are aligned with your truth, for yourself and in your relationships. This concept may sound simple, but for many of us, it is incredibly challenging.

Why, you ask?

Well, by now, you won't be surprised to learn that our family of origin sets our standards for boundary health. Meaning, if your trust was broken in childhood or your boundaries were violated, your internal boundaries today might be shaky. Having one or both parents break promises to you, neglect, mistreat, or abuse you can create disordered internal boundaries that persist into adulthood.

With unhealthy internal boundaries, you might be too easily swayed by others' desires and expectations (for example, repeatedly partaking in a booze-fest when hanging with heavy-drinking pals, even though you promised yourself you'd abstain). Or you might start courses, trainings, or projects only to find a reason to drop out before completing them. Or you might make repeated promises to your partner/sister/pal to start or stop an undesirable or aspirational behavior that you fail to keep. Or not communicate directly when someone behaves inappropriately or crosses a deeply personal line.

TRUE TALK *Self-abandonment is one of the main symptoms of damaged internal boundaries.*

BACK TO YOU:
Keeping Your Word to Yourself

Right now, do a quick inventory of where you don't keep your word to yourself. Increased awareness from this assessment will help you to show up for yourself more consistently.

- Do you make excuses to yourself?

- Do you use language that is inaccurate? Do you say ten minutes but mean an hour?

- Do you overpromise?

- Do you proclaim you will change unhealthy habits and fail to follow through?

- Are you easily swayed by someone else's opinion, thoughts, judgments, or criticism?

- Are you indecisive?

- Do you set goals often to abandon them within a few weeks?

- Is it difficult for you to speak your truth if you know others will disapprove or disagree?

If you answered yes to at least half of the questions above, your internal boundaries need strengthening, so stay the course! Showing up for yourself matters because *you* matter.

Changing these patterns takes time, but the most important element to your success is setting your intention to *stop* abandoning yourself. Slow down and create more internal space with mindfulness and meditation (as discussed in chapter 6) to help you recognize when you are about to slip into old behavior. That moment is your decision point, your fork in the road, where you can continue on with your familiar habits or choose differently. In strengthening your internal boundaries, these moments of choice are *crucial*. Will you do the same old thing, even though you know it won't get you the results you want? Or will you consciously choose new, more self-affirming behavior? Keep your big picture in mind, focus on small steps, and celebrate every time you choose the new behavior. Choosing *not to abandon* yourself (or damage your relationships) not only strengthens your internal boundaries but also builds your self-esteem.

Like many of us, Maria's damaged internal boundaries were reflected in the conflict she was having with herself. I could understand why she was so torn. Keeping the familiar boundary dance alive was not only comfortable, she also knew that Gus making her crumb cake and treating her to Italian food was in line with how he had always shown his love to her. But eating crumb cake and *quattro formaggi* pasta (does any dish need *four* cheeses?) did not serve her ultimate goal of losing weight to feel better. So were these gestures really loving after all? Not really. It was her job to tell him that.

Next up we needed to prepare Maria to get stronger in her healthy desires and to stop abandoning herself every time Gus whipped out the flour. She really wanted him to be her partner in her health, as much as he was her partner in every other area of her life.

Focusing on the big picture made it easier for Maria to stop chastising herself every time she gave in. (Hello, Inner Mean Girl Committee.) She began to remind herself that small steps were the way to truly change their boundary dance. When she still said yes though she really wanted to say no, she saw it as an opportunity to explore what was happening in her body. How did it *feel* to abandon herself? Could she recognize these feelings and sensations as signals for her to get curious? Could she stop long enough to choose the healthier behavior? Once Maria was clear that her own internal boundaries could be fortified, she felt more hopeful about enacting change with Gus.

TRUE TALK *When you have healthy internal boundaries, you can consistently rely on yourself to do what you say you're going to do and feel peaceful knowing that you can take care of yourself.*

The Change-Back Maneuver

That Gus sabotaged her efforts after initially agreeing to support her is a classic *change-back maneuver*. Reactionary and almost always unconscious, the change-back is an attempt to resist change and reinstate the status quo. Maria's move to get healthier was upending their established dynamic, and Gus's behavior sent a clear message: *Not a fan of your latest health kick, Maria.*

In different situations, the change-back might be conveyed with expressions such as, "You're taking this vegetarian thing too far. I am worried it will make you sick." Or "Therapy has changed you. You're no longer the happy/sexy/nice woman I fell in love with."

Whether the change-back is expressed with words or behavior, the intention is the same: to undermine whoever set a boundary or stated a clear desire for change. If you are on the receiving end of a change-back move, know that this tactic may not be coming from a place of malice. Change-back maneuvers can be unnerving, but it's worth pushing through your discomfort to understand the deeper motivation for whatever resistance you're encountering. There is massive power and deepened intimacy to be gained by calmly standing your ground.

Maria knew that Gus was a decent guy. He was not the type to intentionally sabotage her. So she wasn't going to lead with,

"WTF, Gus? I'm on to your crumb-cake game!" Instead, Maria wanted to understand why Gus unconsciously wanted her to stay the same.

Most likely, Gus feared losing her. What if her weight loss changed her so much that she lost interest in him? The woman he knew had been 50 to 80 pounds overweight their entire relationship. What if a new-and-improved, healthier Maria wanted to be with a new-and-improved someone else?

Going Deeper to Create a Brand New Dance

Understanding that Gus was pulling some serious (albeit unconscious) change-back maneuvers was a good place to start. Knowing that Gus's behavior was likely driven by fear, not malice, informed Maria's Proactive Boundary Plan. But we still had to do some further digging into Maria's past. How had *she* come to participate in this unhealthy dynamic? After all, Maria herself had been allowing Gus's unconscious fear to impact *her* well-being. Like so many bad boundary dances, this two-step served no one.

Maria grew up in a defensive family system where people were hyper-sensitive to criticism and didn't have the skills to discuss things openly. Instead of talking, they held grudges or expressed displeasure passive-aggressively with sarcasm or teasing. This resulted in Maria becoming overly compliant in adulthood to avoid conflict, which—surprise, surprise—affected her ability to speak up with Gus.

How you were treated and the model of behavior you witnessed in childhood chiefly determine how you respond to perceived criticism as an adult. If your parents punished you harshly for mistakes or shamed you regularly, you might have developed an ingrained response to negative feedback, like deflection or denial, as a protective mechanism. An instinct for self-preservation can, in turn, trigger defensiveness when someone expresses anger, frustration, or disappointment to you. The adaptive behaviors in childhood (like prioritizing the needs of a volatile parent over your own) become *major* blocks to intimacy in adulthood. Such behaviors shut down authentic, mutual sharing and set the stage for futile conflict, not collaboration. How's that for a lose-lose proposition?

Growing up, Maria's family was very close, allowing little personal privacy. The unspoken, codependent rule to avoid difficult topics left them all with a lot of unexpressed feelings. Then, they used food to numb those feelings. For example, when Maria was upset with her mother, instead of talking things out, her mother would make her favorite crumb cake. (Yes, Gus made the exact same recipe, passed down from his MIL.) Maria remembers her mother standing over her saying, "Eat! It'll make you feel better."

Instead of learning to identify and effectively communicate her feelings and boundaries, Maria was taught to literally stuff her feelings with sweet treats and other comfort foods. Having dessert was a form of self-soothing, modeled by her mother, who also ate sweets when she was upset. Seeing the connection between the present (not honoring her feelings) and her past (eating her feelings) was *crucial* for Maria to change her boundary dance with Gus.

There was a cultural context to consider, too. Maria and Gus both came from big Greek families, where feeding people represented love and affection. So if Maria refused Gus's food, she feared he would be hurt. The thought of causing him pain was unbearable. Although to the outside world, Maria presented as a positive, optimistic, and carefree woman, in fact she was deeply insecure and tended toward approval-seeking behavior. This further hindered her ability to draw effective boundaries with Gus and others. She needed to get clear that how others, including Gus, responded to her stating her needs was *not* her responsibility. It was not her side of the street. Her responsibility was to know, state, and negotiate for her needs.

Armed with real data, we began building her Proactive Boundary Plan. We wanted her to take ownership of her well-being and succinctly express a simple request: that Gus's words and actions

supported her healthy lifestyle (cut the crumb-cake crap, lover!).
She would also reassure him of her commitment to their marriage,
no matter her weight.

Boundary First-Timers and Repeat Offenders

Before we apply our theoretical understanding of boundaries to
your life in practical ways, we need to understand the two different
types of people that many of us deal with: the *Boundary First-Timers*,
like Gus, and the *Repeat Offenders*.

Boundary First-Timers are people to whom you have never actually expressed a boundary request with words. This might include
a coworker who thinks nothing of asking you to weigh in on his
marital conflicts (when you're neither a counselor nor his buddy).
Or a sister who repeatedly borrows your favorite cocktail dress
without your consent. You may secretly think of these people as
self-centered boundary bullies who take advantage of you. But
there could just as easily be other reasons. They might be clueless or
tone-deaf, missing your subtle hints. Or they could be in denial of a
reality they don't like. Maybe they're interpreting the fact that you
don't call them out as consent. Whatever kind of boundary interaction it is, you have not yet given them a chance to change their
behavior. To do this, you need to clearly and calmly make a simple
boundary request. Their reaction to your request will provide valuable data about what they really think and feel.

Repeat Offenders are different. They are people to whom you
have stated your boundaries, and yet they continue to cross the line
that you have explicitly drawn. They plead ignorance, have a selec-
tive memory, or even attempt to talk you out of your own boundary.
Think: the partner who dismisses your dislike of his harem of exes
by telling you that your insecurity is the problem. Or an incon-
siderate colleague who leaves you waiting for 15 minutes outside
an appointment, as usual, and says, "I had to stop quick to return

something to a store that was on the way; thanks for waiting," even though you had specifically requested advanced notice of scheduling changes. When dealing with Repeat Offenders, you need to add specific consequences to your boundary requests, which we'll address in the Power of Consequences section below.

It can be tempting to get super frustrated with the Repeat Offenders, especially if there's still unresolved material in your basement about not being seen or heard as a child. Deep breaths, honey. This person *could* be a Boundary Destroyer, someone who has either no interest or ability to consider your true feelings (a concept we'll cover in chapter 9). But you won't know that until you add consequences to your boundary request and then follow through.

TRUE TALK *When you change the boundary dance in an established relationship, you may encounter a change-back maneuver. This is an unconscious attempt to resist change and reinstate the status quo.*

Whether you're dealing with a First-Timer or a Repeat Offender, your job is to stay dialed in to your own feelings and goals. Remember, when you introduce new moves to any boundary dance, your dance partner is going to notice. Some will be grateful for the new instructions, and some won't. Don't let your decisions get derailed by your fear of the other person's response. This point is vital for your success.

Many of us, especially HFCs and empaths, have been habituated to be all about other people. One of the biggest boundary obstacles is a hyper-sensitivity to being rejected. In asserting your preferences, desires, and deal-breakers, it's crucial to understand that the other person's resistance or reaction is *their* side of the street. Meaning, it's their responsibility. Focus on *yourself*. Although it might be tempting to do a deep psychological analysis of what the other person might be experiencing, it's not going to further your long-term goals of self-empowerment. (Not to mention that *their* mental health is definitely on *their* side of the street.)

Being prepared for some pushback is prudent. You can handle it. Don't read their response (verbal or otherwise) as a signal to abort. Stay the course and have faith. Remember, change happens step by step. Just keep putting one foot in front of the other. One small shift at a time, and your Boundary Boss training will pay off in your future happiness.

Creating Your Proactive Boundary Plan

Your Proactive Boundary Plan is informed by your unique history, life experience, and natural boundary style. You craft different plans depending on each particular relationship and whether or not you're dealing with a Boundary First-Timer or a Repeat Offender. You may also want to take into account the best time to speak with someone. For example, if you know your boss is cranky before she eats lunch, wait until after lunch to speak with her about taking time off.

Now, let's look at the steps in crafting your Proactive Boundary Plan.

Step One: Be Specific About Your Boundary. Get clear about your desired boundary. It is not enough to want things to be different. If you find yourself wishing that a loved one was more "sensitive," challenge yourself to get more specific. Perhaps what you really want is a specific acknowledgment.

For example, instead of complaining to your partner that you both "need to be better with money," make a specific suggestion that you both agree to not make any purchases over a designated amount without consulting the other.

Specificity creates a much higher probability of being understood and potentially getting your needs met, and so it's mandatory to internally clarify what you want in specific terms.

Step Two: Take Stock of Yourself. Get introspective about any unconscious material (yours) that might still be charged and fueling the bad boundary. Use the 3Qs tool from chapter 5. Ask yourself: Who does this person remind me of? Where have I felt like this before? Why or how is this behavioral dynamic between us familiar to me?

The 3Qs quickly clue you in to any transference-related reactions that might be clouding your ability to see the situation clearly. Making the unconscious conscious frees you to make a boundary request based on the facts of the current situation, unmuddied by unresolved historical injuries.

Step Three: Visualize the Empowered Outcome. Visualize how you want your boundary conversation to go. It's crucial that you step out of fear. Focus on the good stuff. It's *awesome* to be seen and heard. It's *wonderful* to have the courage to stand up for being authentically known.

Visualization is a tried-and-true technique, used by top-level athletes to enhance their performance outcomes. This psychological prep work creates the optimal conditions, internally and externally, to successfully make the boundary request. Since we only have control over ourselves, speaking up and clearly asserting our desired boundaries is the goal. The other person's response will reveal what they are willing or capable of doing. For example, if someone is unwilling to compromise, uninterested in the way you feel, or offended that you had the nerve to assert yourself, you will have the opportunity to respond appropriately and perhaps rethink the relationship.

Your feelings and expectations powerfully influence your desired outcomes. The secret to creating what you want, whether a successful boundary request or anything else, is visualizing and *feeling the feelings* of having it. This involves using all of your senses while visualizing: sight, smell, taste, touch, and hearing.

Step Four: Use Direct Language. Create a script using concise, direct, and appropriate language. Depending on the situation, your goal is to inform the other person of your preference, desire, request, or limit, and in some cases, your deal-breakers.

For example, you might say, "I'd like to make a simple request that when you borrow the car, you bring it back full instead of empty." Or "I wanted to bring it to your attention that your texting throughout our family meeting today was distracting to me. I'd like to request that at next week's meeting you abide by our agreed-upon rules and leave your phone in your room."

TRUE TALK *Since we only have control over ourselves, speaking up and clearly asserting our desired boundaries is the goal. The other person's response will reveal what they are willing or capable of doing.*

You do not have to give context when making a request or setting a boundary (you were distracted, which was *distracting*). However, in some cases, extra information can help the other person better understand where you're coming from (wanting to keep agreements and all be present for the meeting).

Be careful, though, that in offering up extra info, you're providing context and not attempting to convince them of your right to institute a boundary. You do not need to convince anyone of that (except yourself, and here's your friendly reminder: *it's your right to talk true*). Giving context is simply adding a layer of information to help the other person better understand you and your boundary request.

Step Five: Express Gratitude. Recognition and gratitude are essential to the success of your Proactive Boundary Plan. Positive reinforcement of new behaviors increases the likelihood that they will continue. A simple statement, such as this one, can increase the goodwill between you: "I appreciate you checking with me before committing to plans with Betty. Your consideration really makes me feel seen and loved. Thank you." The more goodwill, the more appreciated both people feel, the more flexible and durable the relationship becomes.

Love and Boundaries

In Maria's case, even though she resented Gus's interference and knew it was dysfunctional, she still felt guilty for "rejecting" his way of loving her with crumb cake and pasta.

That guilt had nudged her to collude with the least healthy part of Gus. If she could opt out of that unhealthy dynamic, she would also stop *him* from encouraging her to abandon her efforts to become healthier. This positive perspective helped Maria get pumped. She saw a possible win-win for both of them.

Making a boundary request in simple, straightforward terms would allow her to stand up for the highest potential of the relationship, regardless of whether Gus met her request with resistance. Maria's increased boundary intelligence would inevitably spill over into her marriage and hopefully create an opening for both her and Gus to interact at an elevated, more authentic level, deepening their intimacy. After all of our work together, there was just one question remaining: Was Gus flexible enough to tolerate the change and learn a new boundary dance?

As women, we're often taught, "If you don't have anything nice to say, don't say anything at all." The overt and covert message is clear: *Don't complain! Be compliant! (Don't complain when you blatantly took credit for my idea in the meeting today, Bob? Really?)* We can clearly see how this lesson harms us. But even then, we can sometimes have a difficult time changing course and speaking our minds.

When you get down to it, one of our most essential needs as human beings is to be understood. Feeling misunderstood and not known in a relationship or in life can lead to deep feelings of despondency. Loneliness can be a precursor to depression and even suicidal thoughts or feelings. The most excruciating feelings of loneliness can occur in relationships where you are misunderstood. Or worse, where your feelings don't matter. All the more reason to speak up, my dear.

TRUE TALK *Proactive Boundary Plans give you the tools to anticipate situations in existing relationships and to change boundary dances with Boundary First-Timers and Repeat Offenders.*

Becoming fluent in the language of boundaries is *the* bridge to deeper, more fulfilling experiences in all of your relationships. Building your unique boundary scripts and speaking them aloud (to yourself in a mirror or with a pal) before you have the conversation can remove some of the charge. The more you do it, the easier and more natural it becomes. Here we go!

Finding the Right Words

When working on building Proactive Boundary Plans, my clients have reported the most challenging step is sometimes finding the right words. In chapter 10, we will cover real-life scripts and scenarios, but you can start to think through this issue right now. Why wait?

One important truth is that you don't need the perfect words or to execute it perfectly. It's okay to do it messily, badly, or while sweating profusely. In the beginning, you gotta just do it—perfectionism be damned.

The purpose of your boundary script is to construct a statement using appropriate, clear language to inform someone of an issue or desire. The steps below are based on the four-part Nonviolent Communication Process developed by Marshall B. Rosenberg, PhD.

State the issue. If the current situation just happened, you can start by alerting them to your issue, "I would like to talk to you about how you use my spare key to borrow my things without asking me."

State your feelings. Next, move into your feeling state. "I've been looking for my favorite shawl for two weeks and am frustrated that you're only telling me now that you took it for your trip without checking with me first."

Make a simple request. Then, say what you need in a casual, nonconfrontational way. According to Rosenberg—author of *Nonviolent Communication*, the seminal text on conflict resolution—all requests can be simple. Further, you can attach a mutual benefit to the clear, simple request. For example, "I'd like to make a simple request that in the future, if you would like to borrow something of mine that you ask me first, so we can continue to share our clothes [benefit] and avoid ruining our weekly sister time by arguing [benefit]."

Suggest an agreement. Next, suggest an agreement. "Can we agree that if you are interested in borrowing any of my things that you will ask me first?" A shared agreement is a way of engaging and enrolling the other person to take equal responsibility for the success of the new boundary dance.

You will likely need to restate your boundary preference or limit multiple times, even with those who are open to complying. Ingrained behavioral patterns take time and repetition to transform because they require us to be aware *every time* so that we can consciously choose the new action. That's hard for most of us to do.

One study conducted by Harvard psychologists Daniel Gilbert and Mathew Killingsworth found that people are not focused on the outside world nor on what they are currently engaged in nearly 50 percent of the time. This phenomenon is referred to as "mind wandering." According to their Harvard Medical School article, mind wandering serves an important purpose, namely, reducing anxiety. The same brain circuits that are responsible for mind wandering also help us retain our sense of self and understand what others are thinking more accurately.

The takeaway for your boundary success is understanding that the person you are attempting to create a new boundary dance with is not conscious enough almost *half* the time to choose a new action. So patience is definitely in order.

The Power of Consequences

For a Repeat Offender, there is an additional step of adding consequences when they ignore repeated requests. Creating and clearly stating consequences can motivate the other person to respect your boundaries, which, in turn, protects you. You might say, "I have made the simple request that you ask me first if you want to borrow something of mine. You agreed to this a month ago, after you borrowed my steamer without asking. I would really appreciate you keeping your word. If this happens again, I will need to take back my apartment key."

With Boundary First-Timers, you don't need to add an expressed consequence. Instead, start by being transparent about your limits and preferences. You might be pleasantly surprised at the effect your communication has.

In Maria's case, she could tack on a consequence if stating the mutual benefit of getting healthier together didn't motivate Gus to cut the carb crap. For example, "If you continue to offer me food that is counter to my weight-loss goal, I will prepare my food separately from yours." That may not sound like much of a consequence to some, but in their family system, food is synonymous with love, so separating herself in this way would carry significant meaning.

The consequences that you state should be commensurate to the boundary violation and the level of pain or discomfort it causes you. Someone repeatedly stealing money from your wallet should not be given the same consequence (jail) as someone who is repeatedly twenty minutes late to meet you (not making plans with them anymore). We need to choose our battles wisely and accept that compromise is a fundamental part of a flexible, healthy, durable relationship.

TRUE TALK *Being consistent with your behavior is imperative. Boundaries that are enforced inconsistently don't work.*

As humans, pain or discomfort is commonly the driving force behind behavioral change, which is why consequences may be appropriate. This is evident in the behavior of kids. You can tell a child a thousand times that the stove is hot, but they may still remain curious enough to find out for themselves. If they get burned one time, it is highly unlikely that they will touch a hot stove again.

As with parenting, the success of adding consequences depends heavily on your follow-through. If you are serious about setting and enforcing healthy boundaries in your relationships, you must do what you say you're going to do. Consistency is queen. Boundaries that are enforced only some of the time eventually fail.

Walking the Talk

By the time Maria and I completed our proactive boundary-setting prep, she had already begun sharing some select self-realizations with Gus. He was responding with sincere interest and support. Because Maria had never directly requested that he not make crumb cake or a reservation at their Italian place before, Gus was a Boundary First-Timer. She hadn't even expressed how these unwanted gestures made her feel. With her newfound understanding and ownership of their dysfunctional boundary dance and her role in it, she felt less resentment and more motivation to be understood.

In the weeks leading up to the conversation, Gus seemed to sense the energetic shift in his wife. There was nary a peep about cake or pasta. When the time came to talk, she was nervous but hopeful.

Her request led to a long, healing conversation. She pointed out his change-back moves, with the understanding that he had not been intentionally sabotaging her. Just the fact that she could open up that kind of conversation was *huge*. Maria shared with Gus what she had learned about her family of origin and about her own tendency to equate food with love. Gus, in turn, was relieved for the opportunity to talk openly about their unspoken boundary agreements and shared his fear about potentially losing her if she got "too ripped." He committed to supporting her health goals in the specific ways she requested.

Creating their new boundary dance was not without its rocky patches. But Maria learned that Gus was indeed flexible enough to do a new boundary dance, no separate meal prep required. Inspired by Maria's growth, he actually entered therapy himself about a year after Maria started her Boundary Boss journey. Maria's genuine courage and efforts inspired her husband.

Proactive Boundary Plans must be tailored to specific relationships. There really is no "one size fits all" when it comes to effective boundary strategies. Just as Maria and Gus built a new boundary dance based on their unique relationship, desires, and life histories, you will do the same, step by step, putting into action the new tools and strategies you have added to your BB skill set. Next up, things are getting real, lovebug. Yipeeee!

▶ BOUNDARY BOSS IN ACTION ◀

1. **Top of Mind.** Pay attention to how you respond in the moment when a boundary has been crossed. Do you ignore it, address it, explode in anger, or do something different? Observe yourself with curiosity, not judgment.

2. **Go Deeper: Communication Integrity.** Having integrity with your word is a Boundary Boss staple, not to mention a game changer in relationships. Go to page 247 in the "Go Deeper" section at the back of the book to gain clarity on where you might be sabotaging your ability to talk true.

CHAPTER 8

Things Are Getting Real

PICTURE IT. THE YEAR WAS 1997, and I was approaching my graduation from New York University's School of Social Work. Having worked on my boundary skill set diligently, I was very close to becoming a Boundary Boss. In fact, I thought I *was* a Boundary Boss.

I made my preferences and desires known to everyone in my friend circle. I opted out of splitting the bar tab when I didn't drink. I artfully put a stop to the steady stream of auto-advice that one of my besties was prone to offer, "Love ya, Jenny, but I really just need a sympathetic ear, please." This resulted in deeper, more satisfying friendships, and a whole lot more self-respect.

As a new therapist, I created a proactive client agreement, which clearly spelled out my rules of engagement, including payment and cancellation policies. I told clients early and calmly that they needed to give me 24-hour notice or else be responsible for paying the full amount of their canceled session. Being proactive with my boundaries gave me the power to preemptively avoid situations that were not in my (or my clients' and loved ones') best interests.

On the whole, I was learning from mistakes and felt confident and hopeful about living life on my terms. I'm a self-directed, independent Aries at heart, so if you know anything about astrology, you can imagine how incredibly liberated I felt.

Until I didn't.

One homework assignment from my therapist, and my sense of empowerment evaporated. I came face-to-face with ground zero of my disordered boundaries. The assignment? Speak honestly with my father.

Rubber, meet road.

Two Steps Forward, One Step Back

The *getting real* phase of the Boundary Boss process is very common. I see it time and time again with my clients and students. Bit by bit, they are implementing better boundaries. They start to make simple requests to their clients, friends, and lovers. Once they get going, no preference or desire is too small to express. Lasagna over hamburgers. *Frozen II* instead of *Die Hard III*. Leaving a social function early instead of counting the seconds until the rest of the gang is ready to depart. And so on. Slowly, but surely, their world is aglow with infinite Boundary Boss–driven possibilities. Yeah! Becoming a Boundary Boss is *amazing*.

Then they come to an obstacle that feels insurmountable. A brick wall, if you will.

This is normal. In addition to the In-Between you learned about in chapter 6, every new level of boundary skills contains its own mini In-Between. We take two steps forward and one step back. This doesn't happen every time you make progress, but when it does happen—and, heads up, you can bet it will—you may feel deflated.

TRUE TALK *The In-Between is a stage in the Boundary Boss journey when resistance to your new boundary actions can suddenly crop up—even though you've been doing the work. It may feel like a setback, but it does not spell defeat. Hang in there.*

Please resist seeing the backslides as failures. You've spent way too much time cleaning out your basement to return to your old ways. "Relapse is part of recovery" is a phrase commonly used in addiction recovery and a concept that applies to your Boundary Boss journey, too. So don't give up when your budding boundary skills meet a speed bump.

The truth is, it's easier to be a Boundary Boss with folks you're not as invested in. As you become more self-assured, it's less likely that you'll get triggered by, say, something your yoga teacher says or a stranger in passing. But you can expect that old behavioral patterns will come up when you start flexing your growing boundary muscles with the troupe you've been dancing with the longest, your family of origin. And when you get to a major test, it *will* feel personal.

The best way for me to illustrate this part of the process is from my own deeply personal experience.

Back when I was about to graduate from New York University's Silver School of Social Work, my Boundary Boss-ness felt like a done deal, until I casually mentioned to my therapist that I wasn't going to invite my father to my graduation.

"I see no point," I said confidently.

My therapist asked, "Terri, why do you see no point?"

As we have now established, old habits can die hard. When she asked me that direct question, I didn't even blink before speaking.

"Trust me, he won't come," I said emphatically. "He despises Manhattan."

Truth was, her question had rattled me (or to be more precise, her question had rattled my inner child who was still, apparently, afraid of risking my father's rejection).

TRUE TALK *The inner child is the part of us that is stuck in the past, still expecting the reactions and responses she experienced as a child.*

"Okay," she said, thinking for a moment before she added, "but regardless of *his* thoughts, do you *want* to invite him?"

Again, I answered without thinking.

"Yes, of course. He's my father."

Deep down, I really wanted my dad to share in this momentous accomplishment. Given the sacrifices I'd made and the fears I'd overcome to make this major life leap, I was super proud of myself. As graduation neared, I wanted him to be proud of me, too.

In light of that, a million-dollar question hung in the air: *Why wasn't I asking him to be present for such an important life event?*

My therapist looked me square in the eyes and said, "Terri, your healing comes from having the courage to ask for what *you* authentically want regardless of what the other person does. You inviting him is about you honoring your truth—not about whether or not he'll accept."

Looking back, I can see that this was a defining moment for me. Her response completely changed my understanding of boundaries. I saw that inviting him was yet another way to honor my truth and myself. This wasn't about controlling his response. This was about having the courage to finally assert my grown-up self with my father.

You, too, can expect a shift in mindset as you continue to tackle your toughest boundary challenges. Usually, you'll know when staying silent is no longer an option. You'll feel it in your gut. Your chances of success shoot through the roof when you realize that whatever you're about to say or do is all about *you.*

Breaking the chains of high-functioning codependency and disordered boundaries takes grit. This is where you'll be required to dig deep into your own well of courage, as you just might encounter some powerful Boundary Bombs.

Boundary Bombs

When you're developing your BB skill set, be on the lookout for Boundary Bombs, which are forms of self-sabotage that derail your best efforts of creating, maintaining, and enforcing healthy boundaries.

The major ones are the Blame-Shame-Guilt Trifecta, the Boundaryless Hangover, the Boundary Reversal, and the Victim-Martyr Syndrome.

Boundary Bombs can show up at any point on your Boundary Boss journey, but as things get more and more real, the Boundary Bombs might be especially intense. Learning what they are can help you to watch out for them and be prepared.

Boundary Bomb #1: The Blame-Shame-Guilt Trifecta

Blame, shame, and guilt—did your skin crawl just hearing those words? None of these emotional states are pleasant. When it comes to your Boundary Boss learning curve, though, they are also counterproductive and complicating. They derail your ability to draw healthy boundaries.

Blame, shame, and guilt are the fear-driven emotions that kick up defensiveness and erode self-respect and self-esteem. They are very common, and also tricky to navigate. We don't want to get into trouble or be punished, so we deflect and debate instead of having a constructive dialogue. But debating doesn't allow us to listen with the intention of understanding. How can you listen when you're simply trying to crush another person's perspective with your airtight argument?

Insisting you are right may seem like it shields you from blame, shame, and guilt, but actually it just cuts off any chance of having a productive conversation. Oh, and PS, suppressing those unpleasant feelings will only mean that you'll have to head back to your basement with a bucket of Pine Sol at some point.

TRUE TALK *When things get real and you start changing your boundary dances you will likely encounter anticipatory fear. It's important to remember that you can still choose to speak truthfully.*

Blame usually indicates a particular sensitivity to a fear of judgment. When you blame others, *they* get stuck holding the bag, at least in your mind. When you habitually blame yourself, you pre-empt anyone else blaming you first, which creates the illusion of control.

Fears about being judged can indicate deep-rooted feelings of shame, a core belief that there is something inherently wrong with you. Shame (like envy) is so unpleasant that you might not even realize it is a box in your basement. Unexamined and unhealed, it will continue to damage your self-esteem and self-worth.

Many people get confused about the difference between shame and guilt, so let me clarify: guilt feels like you *did* something wrong, while shame feels like *you*, as a person, are wrong.

Shame commonly stems from childhood experiences. Although most of us experienced things that made us feel temporary shame in childhood, persistent shame in adulthood usually originates from chronic abuse or neglect a long time ago. Shame feels hope-less, like there is something fundamentally wrong with you that cannot be fixed.

Healthy guilt, on the other hand, can actually motivate us toward positive action and self-correction. It has a level of redeem-ability that shame does not. If you feel guilty, you can make amends, apologize, or take responsibility for your actions, bol-stering your self-worth in the process. We all make mistakes, and there is something freeing about owning up to whatever needs to be cleaned up.

Unhealthy or toxic guilt is a different beast. It is related to disor-dered internal boundaries, such as taking on guilt for other people's feelings or situations, which you have no actual control over. This is common for those who have grown up in chaotic or dysfunc-tional homes, where children feel responsible for everything. They may think, *If Dad is angry, it must be my fault, and therefore I am bad.* As you can imagine, these painful childhood experiences become ingrained and keep us in survival mode. Which is exhausting.

BACK TO YOU:
Recognize the Blame/Shame/Guilt Trifecta

When blame, shame, or chronic guilt crops up, it's actually a legit opportunity to heal old wounds. As energy medicine expert (and my bestie) Lara Riggio likes to say, "Upset is access."

The key to taking full advantage of this opportunity is to first recognize when you are in the midst of the blame/shame/guilt swamp. Consider these questions:

- Do you find yourself stressing about things that are completely out of your control (even though from every angle, you're not responsible for fixing whatever is happening)?

- Does negative self-commentary such as *I'm a bad person, a fraud, selfish,* or *unlovable* regularly loop through your mind?

- Do you seek temporary relief from unwanted feelings of shame, blame, or guilt in numbing behaviors (food, alcohol, drugs, sex, etc.)?

These are a few behaviors to be on the lookout for. They are all opportunities to recognize that you have some charged material that needs your attention. Get curious and use the 3Rs and 3Qs to uncover the original experiences that might be driving your upset.

Shame isolates and separates us from others. Social scientist Brené Brown, who is a shame and vulnerability expert, says that three things keep shame in the driver's seat of your life: secrecy, silence, and judgment. The cure? Understanding and empathy, which help build connection, courage, and compassion. So once you become aware of shame or toxic guilt at play, write about it or talk about it with a compassionate pal and begin to practice self-empathy.

Boundary Bomb #2: The Boundaryless Hangover

For many of my clients, there's an underlying belief that they are required to offer up things they really don't want to, such as deeply personal information or sex on a first date. Revealing too much to someone they just met or getting sexual too soon just because someone bought them dinner (and maybe also felt entitled to the sexual favor) can result in feelings of *I really wish I hadn't done that*. This kind of vulnerability also reflects disordered boundaries.

When is it "too soon" to get physically intimate? Well, that's personal to you and may depend on what experience you want. Most of my female clients, though, are not seeking therapy because they want to figure out how to get some action, but because they want a sustained emotional connection. When it comes to sex, some women prefer to wait a few months. Others are so dialed into the other person's desire that they don't even know their preference—only that they'd like to avoid being rejected.

When it comes to revealing personal information, that's a judgment call, too. For example, a woman in one of my online courses once asked when she needed to share with a love interest that her alcoholic father had sexually abused her. It was a fair question, but from the anxious undertones in her email, I sensed that she wasn't simply asking about an appropriate timeline. More likely, she felt that something about her was innately damaged, and that this person had a right to know. Not so, I told her. I suggested she unpack the reasons she felt compelled to confess her childhood experiences to a virtual stranger who undoubtedly had his own basement filled with unseemly crap.

For others who are more shamed-based, a true confession is a covert maneuver of getting their "stuff" out into the open and potentially accelerating the relationship's demise (which they are unconsciously expecting). If things are going to end badly, you might as well get that over with sooner rather than later, right? Sparing yourself a rejection down the line serves your illusion of control. You might have felt powerless in an earlier dramatic or traumatic life situation, but now you can put on the brakes so you don't have to risk the terror (according to you) of actually being vulnerable. Hello, secondary gain.

TRUE TALK *Secondary gain is the hidden benefit to staying in or creating a dysfunctional situation.*

The antidote to the Boundaryless Hangover is *voluntary vulnerability*—being discerning and thoughtful about how you share your body, your emotions, your history, and yourself with others. For some, abstaining from alcohol or drinking moderately can help them practice voluntary vulnerability. It's harder to keep your mouth shut about a stressful lawsuit or your messed up family when you've been downing shots of Don Julio.

In cases of physical intimacy, voluntary vulnerability in the form of expressed consent (or a vocal *no*) is especially important if you've struggled with people-pleasing or were raised learning to subjugate your wants, needs, or desires to those of the adults in your life. This may be a painful repeating pattern, and so there's no surprise that it would rear its head as things start to get real.

You cannot change your past, but here's what you can do: accept that your childhood wounds are not your fault. You *did not* deserve any bad things you may have experienced. Be vigilant about noticing the ways in which these familiar patterns show up so that you can put a stop to them now and in the future. You can support your ability to be discerning by cultivating a Proactive Boundary Plan (see chapter 7) to manage expectations and weed out the suitors (or anyone for that matter) whose agenda is misaligned with your own. A short, potentially uncomfortable conversation could spare you weeks, months, or a lifetime of bullshit. The more you exercise voluntary vulnerability, the more clarity you'll have about the choices at your disposal.

Boundary Bomb #3: The Boundary Reversal

Sticking to your stated boundaries can be tough when you're getting your boundary sea legs, so to speak. Let's say you make it clear to your boss that you need to be compensated for working overtime instead of being the one to pick up the slack no matter what. You are backed up by law, your company's HR department, and most importantly, your certitude that you *can* take concrete steps to protect your time, energy, and self-respect.

Yet as soon as you speak up, you instantly want to renege. Sound familiar? This is an example of a Boundary Reversal. Yes, it *is* scary to speak up if it's not something you're accustomed to doing. Understood. However, know that adult-you is not scared. Adult-you doesn't feel the need to destroy your best efforts at living an empowered and self-directed life in an attempt to keep the peace. It's the kid in you who is saying, "It's fine. I didn't mean it. I can still work overtime without compensation!" Happens *all* the time.

As we've discussed, when five-year-old you starts calling the shots, your boundary-setting abilities get compromised. The fear of being honest can absolutely feel like a life-or-death situation to the inner child. But, as we covered in chapter 5, *now is not then*; anticipating some degree of discomfort can help you resist the urge to act on your feelings during a Boundary Reversal moment.

If you walk away from setting a boundary feeling anxious or otherwise unsettled, I recommend instituting a 48-hour rule. Wait two days before taking your boundary back. After the waiting period, it is extremely unlikely you will still want to reverse it.

When you can withstand your discomfort with the unknown (which is another way to look at this), you might discover that the people in your life are actually more flexible than you are giving them credit for. And *you're not that fragile, either, love.* You'll likely see that your inner child's doom-and-gloom script regarding the current situation is exaggerated. When you see this, you will more easily withstand your initial panic. (One exception: the dreaded Boundary Destroyer *will* sense your ambivalence and do their best to wear down your shaky no—a phenomenon that we'll cover in the next chapter.)

> **TRUE TALK** *When drawing boundaries, you cannot dictate how the other person is going to respond. Speak up anyway.*

Look, you may always have a sense of others' discomfort, disapproval, or resistance, but you can choose to focus on your side of the street, not theirs. Even after you've reached full Boundary Boss status, you may not love having tough conversations. That is a-okay. With time, repetition, and consistency, your anxiety will lessen, and the impulse to pull a Boundary Reversal will be in your rearview mirror. Taking the actions that you know are right for you will become your new normal. By reframing your entire relationship to boundaries—what's okay and not okay—your desire for a Boundary Reversal will not hold the sway over you it once did. We gotta just keep on keeping on, people.

Boundary Bomb #4: The Victim-Martyr Syndrome

When we feel victimized, we feel helpless. We believe that what we want does not matter and that our actions cannot change any outcome.

Martyrdom is victimhood's fraternal twin. When we are operating in martyr-land, we feel disempowered, too, but the difference is that we tend to keep score. We over-give, don't speak up, then we secretly feel resentment, as if others owe us something.

The victim part of the Victim-Martyr Syndrome came up for me as I prepared to ask my father to come to my graduation. Because I was so self-determined, I definitely did not identify with the word *victim*, and yet I realized there was no doubt that feeling rejected by my father bordered on victim-ish territory. I didn't even consider asking him because I felt sure that asking would not result in his coming.

TRUE TALK *Boundary Bombs are forms of self-sabotage that derail your best efforts at creating, maintaining, and enforcing healthy boundaries. They include the Blame-Shame-Guilt Trifecta, the Boundaryless Hangover, the Boundary Reversal, and the Victim-Martyr Syndrome.*

My therapist helped me to realize that I had longed for a Daddy's-little-girl situation, with warm and fuzzy words of affirmation. Yet statements such as, "You're the apple of my eye," followed by hugs and kisses were not the way my father showed his love. My therapist challenged me to see if I could *feel* loved by the ways he was capable of loving me. I thought about it. Well, he had paid for my undergraduate education, bought me a used car, and always yelled, "Strap in!" as I drove away after visits.

Wow. I realized that it hadn't occurred to me to view his dutiful actions through the lens of love. To me, they felt more obligatory than loving. As long as I wanted him to love me in this very specific and expressive way, I was setting myself up for disappointment and dejection, further cementing a belief that he didn't actually love me.

When we can shift our attention away from how someone is not showing up for us, we expand our minds beyond our own limiting story. This creates the possibility of something better. Obviously, I'm not suggesting you accept whatever someone is able to give you without asserting your needs, preferences, desires, and deal-breakers. I am suggesting that not all perspectives serve our highest good. Shifting my perspective about my father helped remove some of the powerlessness and fear I felt around asking him to my graduation.

The more my therapist and I spoke, the more I realized how deeply I had misunderstood my options within this situation. Namely, I *had* options. My initial thinking had been that the only valuable outcome would be his agreeing to attend my graduation. Without that, I was powerless to get what I desired.

My therapist guided me to understand that, actually, there was great value in simply being heard, seen, and hopefully understood. Forget the daddy-daughter dances. It turns out that what I desired all along was to be heard, seen, and understood.

If you struggle with the Victim-Martyr Syndrome, you may tend to keep score (hey there, martyr) or get entrenched in powerlessness (victim central). But the fix for each is the same: a willingness to look at your life and choices from a fresh perspective and act on your own behalf. For example, because my father didn't express his love in the ways I wanted didn't mean he didn't love me.

Seeing our relationships and lives from a more expanded vantage opens up infinite possibilities for how we can walk through this world. With honesty, increased self-esteem, and a willingness to take responsibility for your needs, you can successfully shift out of helplessness and into empowerment.

Truth Be Told

Once I got clear on all potential Boundary Bombs, my therapist gave me a homework assignment. On my upcoming annual visit to Florida to see my father, I was to invite him to my graduation. Truth is, I probably wouldn't have followed through otherwise. Having a defined assignment spoke to the achiever in me. Failure was not an option.

My therapist's assurance that my "healing was in the asking" became an affirmation I repeated over and over again until I believed it. It was a relief to know I could only be responsible for my words and actions. That's it.

During our weekend visit, we went to garage sales, walked on the beach, and chatted over seafood dinners. When he asked me about my post-grad plans, I could have made my request. But I didn't. Though I thoroughly believed that the healing was in the asking, I was still nervous. Having all the prep, clarity, and Proactive Boundary Plans in the world doesn't mean you won't get nervous.

By the time he was driving me to the airport, I was sweating profusely. I had to ask him—and do it *soon*. I would be letting myself down if I didn't. I had to act.

"Hey, Dad, I have a question for you," I said, nervously looking in his direction.

"Yes?" he said, his eyes steady on the road. "What is it, Ter?"

"I saved a ticket for graduation for you if you can do it."

As soon as the words were out of my mouth, I took a full-body exhale.

He was quiet for a moment and then said sheepishly, "I really can't."

Even just for a weekend, it was too much. His years of commuting into the city from Jersey had left their mark. He hated the chaos, the crowds, the pace, everything.

I said, "Okay, I understand."

"Here comes the guilt," he replied.

At this moment, I could have analyzed why he was responding like this. I had never guilted him a day in my life. More importantly, I did understand.

Instead, I said, "No guilt, Dad. I totally accept that it's too much, but I want you to know that no one can replace you in my life. You're my only Dad and staying connected is important to me."

Wow, I thought when the words rolled out of my mouth. I had done the hard thing, and that hard thing emboldened me to go even further into my truth. I felt so free. My man-of-few-words father didn't say much, but when we hugged goodbye, he held on for a little longer than normal.

After years of withholding my truth, I finally got it. Communicating honestly about desires, preferences, or limits not only changed my boundary dance with others, it changed how I related to and experienced myself—and *that* changed my life.

A Word on No

As we've discussed, respecting the boundaries of others is essential. Please resist writing an entire story about why they've drawn that boundary (*they must not like me*, etc.). When we learn to effectively communicate through the Boundary Boss process, we can use actual words to get our questions answered instead of filling in the blanks with our own deepest fears.

The cleanest *no* I ever received was from my friend Elizabeth. I had invited her to join me on a vacation to Guatemala. She replied, "Not for me. Can't stand Guatemala. Hot weather and me got a bad thing going."

Her honest response was refreshing: clear, direct, and confident. Nowhere in that email did I sense that she was worried about my feelings if she said no. My emotional reality and response were not her responsibility, which brings up an important point.

When we don't talk straight with our truth, we often unconsciously make work for the people we're engaging with. If you add an over-the-top apology or excessively explain yourself when you say no, you are not being clear, direct, or confident. You are sending a message that says: "I feel so guilty saying no, and I believe that my *no* will hurt your feelings and damage our connection." In trying to be "nice," you might be burdening the other person, who may then feel like they have to reassure you for saying no. So not Boundary Boss behavior, beauty.

With Elizabeth, neither of us had to waste time with a bullshit conversation. My reply to her was, "LOL, copy that, sister." That's it.

When you can give and receive a *no* cleanly, you scoop up a ton of additional energy and attention for the things you really want to say yes to.

BACK TO YOU:
Receiving and Respecting No

For HFCs, people-pleasers, and over-givers, another person's *no*, or limit-setting, can feel like a personal rejection. Answer the questions below to come clean to yourself on how well you receive and respect *no* from others:

- When someone says no to your request or offer, do you feel hurt, rejected, or angry?

- Do you get annoyed or frustrated if the advice you've freely given is ignored?

- Do you indirectly express your hurt or frustration with body language (looking away, sighing heavily, etc.) or with a terse reply such as, "Fine, sorry I bothered"?

Your answers will provide valuable information about where to focus your attention. Remember, the way of a true BB is always *progress* not *perfection*. Learning how to receive a no and respect the limits and preferences of others is one more step toward becoming the Boundary Boss you were born to be.

Mourning the Dream

The final and perhaps most poignant part of *things getting real* is the hardest for many people: allowing yourself to mourn. Becoming self-determined is going to bring up some powerful emotions. One of my clients, Jordan, described how it felt to finally speak her truth to her mother after years of acquiescing to her mother's desires and preferences. For years, Jordan had accepted that her mother's needs came first. Jordan had always traveled to meet her mother, went all out for her birthday, and pretty much made herself available for whatever her mother needed. In therapy, she had worked through the years of built-up resentment and found her own voice.

When Jordan finally told her mother that she would like more reciprocity in their relationship, her mother eventually got on board. From that moment forward, their relationship began to flourish, and her mother began asking Jordan how she felt before making assumptions about how Jordan would fit into her agenda.

After Jordan spoke up, though, she went home and cried, which surprised her. When we unpacked her grief in therapy, she said that she was mourning all the years that she had spent abandoning herself, believing that if she could give enough of herself to her mother, she would then feel worthy.

Not gonna lie, at this stage, you may encounter similar feelings. You might start grieving everything that you had hoped would happen with your Herculean efforts to keep everyone else happy and satisfied. This is an important part of getting real and accepting yourself completely.

So don't let anyone (including yourself) "hyper-positive" you into not honoring this incredibly important part of your emotional process. A sober reckoning of your past behavior, wishing you'd known then what you do now, is a powerful path to more self-determination. This could take many forms: relationships you should have ended sooner (or never started), bullshit behavior you should have tolerated less of, or fear-based reactions that set a ball in motion that you now regret. Time is truly the most valuable coin we'll ever spend, and so, yeah, there is righteousness in allowing yourself to feel sad about that pile of missed opportunities in your past. Honoring your truth and your real past experiences is a radical act of self-love—a mandatory exercise for legitimate Boundary Boss status.

There's another layer to mourning, as well, for the childhood we may have wished for but did not actually have. (Heads up: there's a powerful exercise to help with this on page 248.) The way I wished for a different kind of father, you may wish that one or both of your parents were more evolved or capable than they were. But prioritizing your feelings and truly taking care of yourself now can be a corrective emotional experience. Think of it as an opportunity to reparent yourself and provide the consistent nurturing and encouragement you deserve. In essence, we become the good, healthy, present parent we may not have had.

Whatever is coming up for you, allow your feelings to simply *be*. That way, your emotions don't get stuck (remember, you *did* just clean out that basement). Mourning requires a great deal of self-compassion, an attitude of love and care directed inward. Think of it like this: If your best friend hit a rough patch, would you tell her to suck it up? Or that her feelings weren't valid? (I sure as hell hope not.) I bet you'd be more likely to want to be there supporting her through the emotional mud.

Self-compassion is providing that same solidarity, but with yourself.

I love the juxtaposition that psychologist Kristin Neff, cofounder of the Center for Mindful Self-Compassion, makes: "Unlike self-criticism, which asks if you're good enough, self-compassion asks, 'What's good for you?'" As you reflect on and release the Boundary Disaster years, you may want to move your body more, eat nourishing foods, take salt baths, and pretty much anything else that helps you heal in mind, body, and spirit.

In my case, inviting my father to my graduation brought up powerful emotions. In making a firm decision to appreciate the ways in which he did show his love, I made space for who he actually was. In giving myself room to feel *all* my feelings, I was able to recognize that my fear was exaggerated (a child's fear) and to release the limiting beliefs about my father, myself, and my worthiness. This cleared a path for me to respond in a way that honored my authentic preference and feelings plus created the possibility of deepening my connection with my father (the 3Rs in action: Recognize, Release, Respond).

TRUE TALK *Your healing comes from having the courage to ask for what you authentically want, regardless of what the other person does.*

Before things got real, I wouldn't even allow myself to dream about ways to make our relationship better. Somehow it felt fitting that my graduation to become a psychotherapist also marked a graduation into a healthier chapter of internal boundaries.

My inner work had a profound external benefit. My father began to show up for me in ways I had never expected. He started sending me cards with sweet sentiments *just because*. Often, they had the lone words "Love, Dad" scrawled inside. I remember the first one that came in the mail. He had never sent me cards before for no reason, so when I first saw the envelope, I thought it might be an article about what percentage of my income I should be putting into my 401K. We also agreed to institute a weekly Sunday evening call, which was mostly me talking and him listening, but it was still quality time far beyond anything I had previously been able to imagine.

I cherished his awkward, sweet gestures of love and care. I didn't have the daddy-daughter thing I thought I needed, but what I got was *real* and so much better—all because I was willing to do the work and stay in the process, even when that process had given me a bad case of the Florida sweats. When my father passed away six months later, I was extra glad that I had made my request and told him how much he meant to me. Our time in Florida had turned out to be our last. Gratitude with no regrets.

That's my desire for you, too: stay in the process, do the work, and absolutely have faith in yourself. Yes, things are going to get real (and maybe, in some cases, *really* real). I hope you realize what a golden BB opportunity those moments are.

It's work.

And you're waaaay worth it, beauty.

▶ BOUNDARY BOSS IN ACTION ◀

1. **Top of Mind.** Pay attention to opportunities to have compassion for the child in you. Try this quick but powerful exercise. Get a picture of yourself as a child and keep it in a spot where you can see it often (such as the wallpaper on your phone). Every time you look at the photo, practice feeling compassion for sweet little you and everything she experienced as a child. Let go of judgment. Beam yourself with pure love. That child is *you*. She is perfect, and she deserves your love and compassion.

2. **Go Deeper: Mourn the Dream.** In order to make room for what we are creating, we have to honor and release long-held disappointments. To clear a healthy path forward, do the Mourn the Dream exercise on page 248 in the "Go Deeper" section at the back of the book.

CHAPTER 9

Boundary Destroyers

YEARS AGO, WHEN I FIRST met Jasmine, she floated into my office with a calm and peaceful demeanor. It was striking. She had the aura of an angel. Little did I know, Jasmine was in a living hell.

When I asked why she had come, she readily offered up her family background. She had been raised by two extremely self-absorbed individuals, a narcissistic, workaholic mother and a wounded father, who spent all his emotional capital making her mother happy. Neither parent had much time or energy for Jasmine, and she had essentially learned from a young age that it was her job to uphold her family's "perfect" image and not make any waves. I was impressed by how readily Jasmine shared this information. Not only was she direct, earnest, and astute, but she had clearly done her mental health homework. Missing from her life recap, though, was the reason she was sitting across from me at this moment. I asked gently, "Why are you seeking support now?"

Her face clouded over, and she sighed. "I'm in an abusive relationship," she said. "My boyfriend and I live together. Every day is a nightmare."

Jasmine went on to describe her relationship with Tom, whom she met in the gym three years before when Jasmine hired Tom to be her personal trainer. Tom was funny, charming, and, most of all, adoring. He worked hard to impress her. Eventually, she agreed to go on a date. Soon after, he was calling her his dream woman and talking about getting married. Jasmine was over the moon, except for the occasional moment of doubt: *Was Tom too good to be true?*

That thought made her nervous, but Jasmine dove in headfirst anyway. Within three months, they were living together.

Once he moved into her place, his attention waned. He started acting sketchy, too. He often stayed up late, and if she came out to the living room to see what he was up to, he'd casually shut his laptop. Although her gut said otherwise, Jasmine told herself that everything was *fine*.

Then, he became critical, particularly around her food choices. He also snooped in her phone, said snide things about all of her friends, and got jealous when she spent time with anyone else. She felt like she had to distance herself from the people she loved in order to make him happy. By the time she came to see me, his controlling behavior had reached the point of physical violence. If she dared argue with him, he would push her against the wall or throw her on the ground. Making matters worse, Tom appeared to be the perfect partner to outsiders. Who would even believe her?

She said, "I'm done waiting for things to go back to being blissful. It *never* happens."

Tom sounded like a Boundary Destroyer, a specific type of personality who has no ability (or desire, maybe) to respect others. Knowing that he was physically violent, my response to Jasmine's story was clear.

"There are many therapists in New York City who will take your money while you think about leaving this guy. I'm not one of them. If you are ready to make a rock-solid plan to safely remove yourself from this abusive situation, I'm your person," I said. "If not, I am happy to refer you to another therapist."

Jasmine nodded. "I'm ready *now*."

Game on.

When the Rules Don't Apply

Ever encountered someone who has zero ability to listen and consider your preferences, thoughts, or feelings? Meet what I call the Boundary Destroyers. For this especially difficult personality type, your healthy boundaries do not compute, no matter how eloquently you state them.

A Boundary Destroyer is someone for whom *compromise* is a dirty word. They disregard other people's boundaries, whether consciously or unconsciously, overtly or covertly, partly because they feel like they are above limits (and in some cases, actual laws). They are the people who feel entitled to your time, care, and attention and are not concerned with reciprocity.

Boundary Destroyers are highly contentious, reactive, deeply sensitive, and self-absorbed. They *may* fall into the category of Cluster B personality types, which include narcissistic, antisocial, histrionic, and borderline personality disorders. But we are not attempting to diagnose your Boundary Destroyer, or *anyone else* for that matter. (To determine if someone is suffering from any of these personality disorders requires an in-person assessment by a professional—that's not what we're here for.) What's important is for you to identify the common behaviors of these highly challenging personalities and assess how you might be currently engaging with them. Since Boundary Destroyers tend to use predatory behavior to ensure that you'll maintain their status quo, knowledge is definitely power. And please note: your safety *must* be your top concern. This is especially important if your Boundary Destroyer has a history of violence or if they display a callous disregard for your well-being. If you fear for your safety, please seek professional support and guidance. You must be extra vigilant in protecting your interests and well-being due to the *potential* for the Boundary Destroyer to not take your best interests into account at all.

TRUE TALK *Boundary Destroyers will often disregard your boundaries because they feel entitled to your time, care, and attention. They are primarily concerned with their own needs, not yours.*

Attempting to assert your boundaries with a Boundary Destroyer can be frustrating and confusing. Proactive Boundary Plans that are effective with Boundary First-Timers or Repeat Offenders are less so with BDs because the normal rules of engagement don't apply. Trying to reason with one—whether a family member, coworker, romantic partner, ex, or friend—can be crazy-making.

Why? Because Boundary Destroyers tend to be all about themselves and their agendas with excessive self-involvement eclipsing empathy and compassion. Other people matter only to the extent that you can serve their worldview. Their version of reality is the *only* reality.

A few examples of Boundary Destroyer behaviors include

- the insecure mate who picks a stupid fight the night before you have an important presentation at work (or anytime your attention is elsewhere) and then calls you selfish and storms out when you tell him you can't discuss his issue until after your presentation;

- the domineering mother who regularly competes with you, is threatened by your success, and seeks to take credit for your accomplishments;

- the flirty partner who outright denies that he was inappropriate at a party, even though you saw him slip his number to another woman (according to him, you're terrorizing him with your "crazy");

- the coworker friend who justifies padding their monthly expense report saying they deserve and are entitled to the stolen money because they are underpaid and underappreciated;

- the impossible boss who continually ignores your request not to email on weekends or who incessantly texts you while you are on vacation, taking a personal day, or on medical leave.

Many of my clients and students have a tendency to intellectualize the behaviors of the Boundary Destroyers in their lives, making it easier to overlook a major disconnect between what the Boundary Destroyers are saying and what they're actually doing. But please note: the Boundary Destroyers' actions are *always* going to be more telling than their words.

The Cracked Pot to the Cracked Lid

Before we delve into the sneaky maneuvers that Boundary Destroyers employ to get around your boundaries, I'd like to point out something important: if you are a high-functioning codependent (HFC) or a highly sensitive person, you are especially susceptible to the Boundary Destroyer's ploys. While you absolutely do not have to be raised by a Boundary Destroyer to struggle with them in your adult life, growing up in a household where the parents' needs come first (at the expense of the child's well-being) will make you more likely to encounter (and by "encounter" I mean "be tortured by") Boundary Destroyers until you are able to heal the original wound. Whatever your upbringing, the only part of this dance you have control over is your behavior. Understanding why you might be the perfect Boundary Destroyer target is key to stepping out of these toxic relationships.

Especially if you suffer from the disease-to-please, you may be naturally inclined to dial into others' wants and needs. The Boundary

Destroyer can spot your emotional sensitivity a mile away and seeks to leverage your sensitivity to their advantage.

I've seen this phenomenon in my practice plenty, where an intelligent, highly empathic client is caught up in a destructive relationship with a Boundary Destroyer. What's important for you to understand is that the Boundary Destroyer is not like you. Many lack empathy (though some do a decent job of pretending), and some even have no conscience. Since Boundary Destroyers believe that the end justifies the means, they use tactics like love bombing, gaslighting, emotional manipulation, excessive guilt, and lying as control strategies.

If you are an HFC or empath, you probably have a hard time wrapping your head around what it would be like to have no conscience or empathy, not to care that others are in pain or suffering or even consider how your actions might affect them. Your genuine goodness is exactly what the Boundary Destroyer is banking on. (Word to the wise: HFCs also often fall into the category of highly sensitive people. This means having a sensitive nervous system, being acutely aware of subtle mood shifts in the people around them, and feeling overwhelmed when in a highly stimulating environment. You can determine if you are a highly sensitive person by taking a quick quiz online at BoundaryBossBook.com/bonus.)

If you are the target of a Boundary Destroyer's manipulation, you might struggle with feelings of resentment, confusion, and sadness. And since you are prone to overextending yourself, you might give more to the Boundary Destroyer, only to be met with a message, direct or indirect, that you are *still* not doing enough. So you keep trying to fill their bottomless well. But you can never succeed, so you start believing that *you* are not enough. The honest-to-God truth? For Boundary Destroyers, you will never be or do enough because it's not actually about you.

TRUE TALK *Many Boundary Destroyers lack empathy (though some do a decent job of pretending), and some even have no conscience.*

If you are struggling with a Boundary Destroyer, it's vital to understand exactly what you're dealing with before you craft an action plan. This is super important, especially if you're married or share children, property, or a business. The cost of acting impulsively with this controlling and potentially vengeful personality can be high. Once you can identify their underhanded maneuvers and your own boundary deal-breakers, you are in a far more empowered position to act strategically and successfully.

Manipulation Tactics

Master manipulators, Boundary Destroyers set the rules of engagement, which others are then expected to live by. The ways that a Boundary Destroyer can manipulate are plentiful; below are three of the most insidious tactics that Boundary Destroyers employ.

Flipping the Script

Boundary Destroyers are *experts* at taking the focus off of themselves and their shadiness. If you lay down the law with a very reasonable request, "I do not want to stay out past 10 p.m. because I haven't been feeling well, and I need my sleep," the Boundary Destroyer may respond as if you've just punched them in the face: *How dare you!* Their response is a calculated effort to make you change your mind. You expressing needs, desires, and especially limits can set them off.

Another flip-the-script maneuver is to pretend to make you the object of their concern, especially if you're calling out bad behavior. For example, when you are not cool that they stayed out late and didn't bother to call, they counter: "You know, I'm really worried about you.

You seem extra sensitive lately. Is something going on with you?" These maneuvers are straight-up ploys to get you to doubt yourself while taking the focus off of whatever the hell they were up to.

Another variation is getting upset with you for asking a simple question or blowing something you've done out of proportion. If the Boundary Destroyer is doing something sketchy behind your back, they might respond by raking *you* over the coals in a bid to make you defensive and to deflect any potentially negative attention from them. For example, a client of mine called her new lover and said that she was troubled by his evasive communication style (after he'd been in constant, reliable contact the first few weeks). Her honesty prompted him to go on the offensive, saying, "Well, I can't believe you wouldn't tell me this in person. I feel disconnected, too, you know. You're the one who fell asleep last Wednesday night, not me!" He did everything he could to make her second-guess herself, even though her feelings were valid. (And to no one's surprise, he turned out to be a lying sack of shit; she ditched him shortly after this interaction.)

A Boundary Destroyer might split hairs or outright distort what you've said, such as, "I never agreed to talk about the holidays with you *before* making plans with my family. I just agreed to talk about holiday plans with you." Or they might ask you to do one teeny-tiny favor before socking you with something bigger, insisting that you already agreed to do something you absolutely did not. Some may try to invalidate your feelings by responding with a higher-stakes situation (that's actually irrelevant, but can be a successful way to deflect and put you on the defensive). For example, you don't like that your partner accepts middle of the night phone calls from a now-married ex, and when you say so, your partner replies, "Real nice. She has *cancer*." Guess what, though? Her cancer (if she, indeed, has it) is not your side of the street. What is your side of the street is how you feel about midnight phone calls from his ex.

Gaslighting

One of the most pernicious forms of manipulation is gaslighting, in which the Boundary Destroyer seeks to sow seeds of doubt in the targeted individual in order to maintain control in the relationship. With gaslighting, Boundary Destroyers use a stealth arsenal of persistent denial, misdirection, contradiction, and lying, which are employed to make you question your memory, perception, and sanity. If you've been subject to ongoing gaslighting with someone close to you, you may indeed feel like you're losing your mind. For example, when you were a child, maybe you witnessed a dramatic and scary fight between your parents—thrown dishes, World War III level yelling—but after, when you asked your mother why they were arguing, she said, "Oh, we weren't fighting, honey. You have such a wild imagination."

At its heart, gaslighting is an attempt to delegitimize your beliefs and make you question your reality. It involves constantly controlling the narrative, which means negating or denying your lived experience. You may be told that you're too tender or fragile, or maybe *you* question your own levels of sensitivity—*Maybe it's just me.*

Major indicators of being gaslit include being extremely and excessively cautious so as not to upset your partner/mother/boss, feeling compelled to hide what's really going on from friends and family, apologizing all the time, feeling like you can't do anything right. You may also feel drained of your life force, like the usual pep in your step is nowhere to be found.

And why shouldn't you be joyless when someone close to you is attempting to control your reality? Being manipulated sucks. A vibrant sense of self is based on self-trust, a strong connection to your inner knowing. That is your birthright, lovely. Do you know who doesn't give a crap about that? The person gaslighting you.

At first, you may be in shock, like, *Did I make that up? Am I going crazy?* In the beginning, a pattern hasn't yet been established, so as odd as you may find the behavior, it's not a five-alarm fire. As time wears on, you will begin to get very defensive. "I did not say that!" or "You promised that I was next in line for the promotion!" There's a strong need to assert yourself, even on the small stuff, like whether or not you agreed to a barbecue (you freaking did not). And yet, the skilled Boundary Destroyer has a way of wearing you down. They have quite the detailed map of all your shame buttons, and they know just how to push them to keep you silent and subordinate.

Love Bombing

Love bombing is another common tactic of narcissists. They flatter their targets, feeding their ego and fantasy of true-love-always belonging until they are sure they have their victim hooked (and yes, the love-bombing drug is more heroin than ecstasy). At that point, this type of Boundary Destroyer starts being highly critical, disapproving, and hostile. Eventually, disdain turns into total rejection, and they discard you altogether. The narcissistic cycle of abuse has three stages: (1) idolize, (2) devalue, (3) discard.

Understand that, in stage one of this abusive cycle, the Boundary Destroyer's over-the-top attention is driven by their (conscious or unconscious) desire to gain full control over you. Being on the receiving end of love bombing can be very seductive and overwhelming. It's marked by grand, romantic gestures that you only dreamed could happen in real life. Love bombing can occur in other contexts, too, such as in friendships, professional situations, or even in cult recruiting. Victims tend to blame themselves: *If only I hadn't made that fatal mistake, I could once again be held in high esteem.*

A resurgence of flattery and attention happens when the love bomber (the highest order of Boundary Destroyers) senses that you've reached a breaking point. They give just enough to hope.

This was definitely Jasmine's experience. Whenever she'd had enough, Tom would be sweet just long enough to reignite her hopes. She thought that if she gave more and stayed thin enough that she would earn her spot in his good graces again. Similar to a drug addict chasing that initial high to the detriment of everything else. I've seen this cycle of abuse countless times, and it *always* ends badly.

More Manipulation Tactics

Besides flipping the script, gaslighting, and love bombing, Boundary Destroyers also use the following methods to get what they want, which is total control.

Rejecting Your Feelings. A client once told me that whenever she got upset, her husband would say with hostility, "I'm not going to feel sorry for you because you're crying." Like, what? She was feeling her emotions (not asking for his pity), but his response communicated that she had violated one of his unspoken rules: you are not allowed to get upset.

Along these lines, a partner who tries to invalidate your emotions might say, "You're lucky I'm so sensitive. No one else could handle you."

Money. Many Boundary Destroyers use money as a form of covert control, giving gifts or providing financial support to keep you dependent on them. If you are financially dependent on a Boundary Destroyer, you may be more accepting of their abuse because you are worried about how you would cover basic survival without them.

Acting. Some Boundary Destroyers behave as if they are needy or helpless, to con you into satiating their desires. A narcissistic mother, for example, might appear to be distraught in order to get sympathy from her daughter. A partner who senses your weakness may put on a show of feeling rejected and dejected so that you agree to their ideas and plans.

Anger. Some Boundary Destroyers use hostility to wear you down, yelling and sometimes stonewalling. You may feel so weary that you lose sight of the fact that their behavior is abusive and wrong. The moment they sense you're at your wit's end, they will shift gears and act lovingly. Relieved to no longer be the target of their anger, you're more likely to agree, not realizing that they've just played you like a fiddle.

TRUE TALK *The normal rules of engagement simply don't apply with Boundary Destroyers.*

Peer Pressure. Some Boundary Destroyers use peer pressure to convince their targets that they should acquiesce to the Boundary Destroyer's plan. For example, one client told a new love interest that she wanted to wait three months to have sex. On their next date, he reported that the average woman has sex after three and a half dates. Not only did he try to peer pressure her into doing something she stated she wasn't ready for ("normal women do it in this time frame"), but he actually *researched* the topic and attempted to use empirical data to wear her down as well.

Less obviously calculated peer pressure can sound like, "Well, my whole family agrees with me on this one," or "You know what? I defended you when Bob called you selfish, but now I'm beginning to think he was right." Then, you're more focused on Bob's alleged bad-mouthing than the fact that someone you're involved with is insulting you as a means of controlling you.

Observe Their Behavior

The most important thing you can do if you're struggling with this type of self-absorbed personality is to always be observing their behavior. Don't let things slide. Call them out sooner than later, and you will get a lot of good intel from their response to being challenged. Do they sit down and say, "Oh, my gosh. I didn't realize that I was doing that. Tell me more. I want to understand how you feel. You matter to me"? If you're dealing with a Boundary Destroyer, that will not happen, but if it does, you'll get a clear message about how they really feel within the next day or two, when they either repeat the offense they claimed to be unaware of, mock you for your sensitivity, or drop you altogether.

In established relationships, once you've become accustomed to the dynamic, as messed up as it might be, it's harder to articulate and identify why you feel so upset. If your boss/lover/mother/whoever apologizes for behaving inappropriately, that's fine, but most importantly, be on the lookout for *changed behavior*. Words are the Boundary Destroyer's loaded gun, so if you don't want to be held hostage, watch to see if their actions line up with their words. As the saying goes, the best apology is changed behavior. This is especially true for Repeat Offenders, in which case I'd modify that statement to, the *only* apology that matters is changed behavior. Words without changed behavior are simply a continuation of their manipulation. If we accept someone's apologetic words and they continue to violate a boundary, we're now in collusion with their lowest survival instincts. Worst Groundhog Day *ever*.

How It Begins

Jasmine had been living her own horrible Groundhog Day for too long. Before she set foot in my office, she had made the courageous move to tell her best friend what was really going on.

Breaking the silence was the beginning of the end of her collusion with Tom's abuse and propelled her to therapy, but she needed professional guidance to plan her safe escape, which is why she came to see me.

In therapy, Jasmine made the connection between her parents' neglect and her current relationship. Her mother was a narcissist and most definitely a Boundary Destroyer. She would chastise Jasmine if she didn't perform up to her mother's standards and placed a strong emphasis on how Jasmine looked. Was she in the right dress for Sunday service, for example? Her mother had little compassion and no interest in Jasmine's emotional experience. Her mother was, however, very invested in projecting an image of the perfect and enviable family.

Being raised by a narcissistic mother negatively impacted Jasmine's sense of identity and self-worth. Telling her mother no or standing up for her own individuality were not options. Jasmine learned that to be loved she needed to suck up bad behavior and comply with the desires and demands of others.

Shout-out to all the women reading this book who, like Jasmine, were raised by a narcissistic, self-centered, or mean mother. That is a very specific and painful type of Boundary Destroyer abuse. Not having a mother's close, comforting support is very lonely and is exacerbated by the mother-worshipping society we live in. Many such daughters struggle with depression and anxiety, and most feel alienated and ashamed to admit that they felt unloved by their own mother.

If you were raised by this type of mother, I feel you and am witnessing you and your experiences with a ton of compassion. You are not to blame for your mother's dysfunction or behavior toward you. You did not deserve whatever psychological games she played, insults she hurled your way, or any of the abuse you received. As with all Boundary Destroyers, the narcissistic or unloving mother will never be happy, no matter what the child does. She is a far cry from a healthy parent who gives you the freedom to make your own choices and sees you as separate from themselves.

For Jasmine, taking a break from her mother was important while she hatched her escape plan. It made practical sense for Jasmine to be vigilant about limiting exposure to her toxic mother.

If you happen to have a Boundary Destroyer parent, taking space can help you gain immense clarity on all areas of your life, as well as free up energy to take actions that best support your goals and well-being. If you need space, take it.

Limiting the Harm

With non-Boundary Destroyers, healthy limit-setting is a highly effective means of protecting yourself and your relationships. With Boundary Destroyers, though, it's not so simple.

As is common in abusive dynamics, you may be tempted to take more than your share of the blame. You may chastise yourself for ignoring your body wisdom that told you something was off, like those pangs in your stomach or the constriction in your chest. As you reflect, please remember that their charm offensive was part of a larger strategy to control and manipulate. No need to self-flagellate. You are responsible for your behavior, not theirs.

For Jasmine, her realization that her best efforts would not change Tom came only after she was physically abused. Even if your Boundary Destroyer doesn't lay a finger on you, know that emotional and verbal violence are extremely damaging, especially if you are sensitive. Sooner or later, you will reach a bottom, like Jasmine, but everyone's bottom is different and what you do is up to you. Due to the *potential* for the Boundary Destroyer not to take your best interests into account, you *must* be extra vigilant in protecting your interests, safety, and well-being.

To step out of the Boundary Destroyer's manipulative vortex, you need to get clear on the fact that manipulation with the intent to control you is *not okay*. Trusting yourself can be a very steep hill to climb when someone has launched a stealth campaign against your perspective, intuition, and autonomy, but it can be done. Carve out space to develop and strengthen your belief in your own intuition. If something feels off, painful, or constricted in your body, that's your body wisdom piping up, saying, "Pay attention. This ain't right."

> **TRUE TALK** *Since it is unlikely that true Boundary Destroyers will change significantly, it's best to come to terms with that fact. You can use the strategies provided in this chapter to protect yourself from their toxicity, especially if you feel unsafe.*

Meditation will help you get in touch with the stillness within and replenish your own energy. Your self-care really matters, especially in charged situations. You can always step back from a conversation while you gather your thoughts. Breathing deeply will bring you back to center. Learning to regularly use the 3Rs (Recognize-Release-Respond) helps you behave more mindfully so that when someone is attempting to manipulate you, you have enough response time to allow for your own wisdom and truth to guide your action. Your gut is rock solid.

Acceptance is key. You will never win with a Boundary Destroyer. Even if you have the best bullet-pointed argument in the world, the Boundary Destroyer is not going to acknowledge your truth. Convincing them of your perspective is a thankless, energy-zapping task. Once you're clear on that, do what you must to save the only life you can save—your own.

The Boundary Destroyer uses these underhanded tactics because many have an extremely fragile sense of self and deep self-loathing. Most likely, they are afraid that if you were to become more self-confident, you'd leave. Not your circus, not your monkeys—their insecurity is squarely on their side of the street. Stop making choices to assuage their inner wounds. You can't make up for their horrible childhood. But you can start making *conscious* choices that support your well-being, safety, and empowerment.

Jasmine was super clear on her top choice: freeing herself from Tom's grip. She was going to move out and never speak to him again. To do so, she and I put together a careful plan for her to move out while he was away on a business trip. Like her mother, Tom had the tendency to play the victim. So she also had to mentally and emotionally prepare for losing the PR battle with their mutual friends.

Just as it's pointless to try to win with a Boundary Destroyer, it's also a waste of your precious time and energy to convince people to see your point of view. Those who know the real you won't for a second doubt you or your intentions. Others may take the Boundary Destroyer's side, but like Jasmine, you have to let go of caring what others think.

If you are dealing with an abusive Boundary Destroyer, leaving, going no contact, or both are the ideal options. If the Boundary Destroyer is a parent, that can be challenging, but again, no contact *is* an option. Some of my clients press pause on their relationships with a familial Boundary Destroyer for a set amount of time. Distance can be healing and interrupts the boundary dance. Then, if you decide to be back in touch, you are less likely to let them dominate you or push your buttons. Nothing they do is actually about you anyway.

Especially if you are dealing with a narcissist, prepare to deal with their rage if you decide to end the relationship outright. Remember, they feel entitled to control you and may do everything in their power to destroy you for asserting your sovereignty.

You may need to block their number or have a mini-funeral for the relationship you wished you'd had, and then go on living as if they are actually dead to you. Whatever you decide, one thing is certain: you cannot rationalize with them, so don't even try.

If leaving or having no contact is not an option, the Gray Rock method, essentially becoming bland and unreactive, will help you become a less interesting target. Boundary Destroyers aggressively seek your attention to fill their inner emptiness. Seeing you upset is like catnip to them. *Any* charged emotional reaction will replenish their supply. But if you're boring, they get bored, too—with you, which is what you want.

Jasmine used this technique as she waited to launch her escape plan. Tom would come home and make a snide remark, like, "Please tell me you didn't wear *that* dress today," and hard as it was, Jasmine would say with a neutral tone, "I did." Like Jasmine, you have to be disciplined in never tipping your hand, no matter how you feel inside. Eventually, they will look elsewhere for their drama fix.

If you are in a relationship that you cannot simply end—for example, you're raising children together—you *must* take emotion out of your communication. Boundary Destroyers *do not care* how you feel. Lindsey Ellison, author of *Magic Words: How to Get What You Want from a Narcissist*, advises treating communication with narcissists like a business transaction. She has a winning formula to help you get what you need, which involves understanding the narcissist's wounds and insecurities (not being worthy) and then speaking to how they hope to be seen (worthy). For example, "Can you help Johnny with his science homework? You're so good at explaining concepts, and I think he'd love it." Yes, it can be hard to offer up praise to the person who has been tormenting the crap out of you, but remember, this is business. Feed their ego strategically to suit your needs. If you can't manipulate the manipulator, stepping out of the power struggle will, at the very least, keep you calm.

If you are dealing with a dangerous individual, I *strongly* advise that you seek professional help in navigating your situation. It's better and safer to forego a dramatic exit, since there is the possibility that the Boundary Destroyer may decide to make your life a living hell to prove they can still control you. Seek out resources for victims of domestic violence, and craft your exit strategy with careful intention. In some cases, the Gray Rock method may be preferable to a restraining order, because as with certain predators, a legal decree can increase violence. Your safety always comes first, and a skilled professional can help ensure that you are protected.

If you have recently begun a relationship with someone you suspect might be a Boundary Destroyer, test them by pushing back a bit on their plans. For example, if your new love interest says, "I made reservations at an Italian restaurant," don't just say, "Great!" Say, "Actually, I feel like eating Japanese." Boundary Destroyers have very poor impulse control, and even in the early days, you will be able to spot signs of resentment that you dared to challenge their plan. If you can spot trouble early, you are in a far better position to be very firm with your boundaries or hightail it the hell out of there.

If you don't test the waters early, you may wind up in a situation where you're confusing *compliance* with *compatibility*. I once had a client come in to tell me that she was unsatisfied in her "perfect" relationship, though nothing was technically wrong. Her partner was, in her words, "quite particular" about everything. (Read: controlling.) The more we spoke, she revealed that her partner set their social schedule, never once asking what she might like to do. In fact, he didn't even *know* what she liked. Like many women, she went along with his agenda because she hated conflict, which brought her to a very lonely place. Of course, it's lonely to be in a relationship based on compliance, which is characterized by one-sided consideration, nonstop giving, assuaging, and conceding to keep the peace. Continual self-abandonment can be devastating.

No matter how far along you are in a relationship (romantic or otherwise), your experience will start to shift dramatically when you decide to be the boss of you. Your time is valuable, and you decide how to spend it. If you have a Boundary Destroyer who spews abusive comments, let them know in no uncertain terms that you are not going to tolerate that. For example, "I'd like to make a simple request that you not call me 'a bitch' or any other derogatory name anymore. If you do it again, I will hang up the phone." The Boundary Destroyer *will* cross that line again, and what's so key is keeping your word. Even if it feels uncomfortable, you must follow through and not tolerate destructive behavior.

In Jasmine's case, she eventually took a page from Michelle Obama and revised it for her specific situation: When they go low, we get the hell out! With calculation and planning, Jasmine made her move. When Tom was away, she safely removed her belongings from the apartment, blocked his phone and email, and moved across the country. After a period of healing, in which she worked to address childhood wounds so that she would not attract another Tom-type, she met a wonderful partner and has been with him ever since. She established a successful business and is a true success story, moving from Boundary Disaster to Boundary Boss.

If you're exasperated from dealing with a Boundary Destroyer, freedom can be yours, too. Be honest with yourself, don't give up, figure out your next right action and then the next until you are free.

▶ BOUNDARY BOSS IN ACTION ◀

Note: If you are in danger, get help. Prioritize your immediate well-being and make a careful plan to change your situation.

1. **Top of Mind.** Pay attention to where the other person's words do not match their behavior. Boundary Destroyers can be persuasive verbally, but their actions reveal the truth about their ability or intention to really change.

2. **Go Deeper: Boundary Destroyer Hit List.** Snuggle up in your Zen Den and turn to page 249 in the "Go Deeper" section at the back of the book to complete your hit-list exercise.

3. **Get Inspired.** Dealing with Boundary Destroyers is exhausting, so prioritizing your self-care is more important than ever. Draw yourself a luxurious bath, take a 24-hour tech break, eat nourishing food, and fill up your own cup, love. I'll be waiting for you in the next chapter.

CHAPTER 10

Real-World Boundaries
(Scenarios + Scripts)

SUIT UP, BOUNDARY-BOSS-IN-TRAINING! It's time to get down to the nitty-gritty and learn effective boundary scripts you can personalize to use in any scenario.

The freedom and expansion that comes with actually having the right words at the right moment might just blow your mind. In this chapter, we explore boundary-setting in common dynamics that play out in different types of relationships. Use the suggested scripts that follow to craft language with your partner, boss, mother, bestie, or some rando in Starbucks. As you become more confident in your boundary-setting skills, you'll find your own particular wording and delivery style.

But first, let's review your process for boundary-setting to assure maximum success.

Use the 3Rs to Speak with Purpose

By now you know the steps for establishing Proactive Boundary Plans. That means you have the tools to make decisions based on your understanding of existing situations and the people with whom you are establishing new boundaries or changing the existing dance. (Need a refresher? Go to page 135.) As you speak your truth, remember that context is everything. In established relationships, you have a sense of who the other people are and how they might best receive your words, but out there in the world, a Proactive Boundary Plan isn't always possible. That's why, for setting boundaries in any context with any person, the 3Rs (Recognize-Release-Respond) is your general framework in the moment. This three-step strategy helps you clarify a few important things within yourself and then effectively make your request, express your true feelings, or let someone know that a line has been crossed. Here's the review.

> **TRUE TALK** *It's not your job to educate every person in the world about healthy boundaries, but it is your job to create and protect your own healthy boundaries.*

First, *recognize* that there's a problem. You can tell because you feel a bodily sensation that doesn't feel good—for example, a knot in your stomach or a constriction in your chest. Body wisdom *may* be a signal that there is external conflict (with, say, a demanding friend), but it will *always* be a signal that there's internal conflict in you. Body wisdom is your built-in alarm system, alerting you to the fact that you're not comfortable with whatever is transpiring or about to transpire. Tuning in to your genuine, inner experience gives you important data that you can then use to identify the problem.

Second, *release* any historical charge from an old injury or unhealthy influence from your Boundary Blueprint. You may find yourself reacting to an ancient wound, especially if you feel yourself getting upset. You may also find yourself rationalizing another person's behavior, wanting to make excuses for them, instead of focusing on what's true for you. Listen, a boundary violation is a boundary violation. Whether the other party intended to hurt you or not, if their behavior feels harmful to you, you still have a right to speak your truth in the here and now.

Third, *respond* in a way that feels mindful and clear. When you know what the problem is and what you want, you can choose the appropriate words to convey your perspective and feelings precisely. If you sense that Aunt Betty didn't mean any harm with her invasive question about why you don't have kids, you may adopt a kind or gentle tone to get off the topic of your fertility. For example, "That's not on my radar at the moment, but tell me about you. How have you been feeling?" If your coworker is trying to get personal information out of you, you may shut down his questions about your personal life a bit more directly. For example, "Hey Bob, I prefer to keep my personal life *personal*." It's not your job to educate every person in the world on healthy boundaries. It *is* your job to know and protect your own healthy boundaries.

> **TRUE TALK** *Keep in mind that you want your communication to be assertive. It's that sweet spot between being too passive and too aggressive.*

Boundary Scripts 101

Boundaries in action are a *process*. There's no magic pill that ensures a perfect execution. So the tools and scripts that follow help create a foundation to build on. Keep the words that work (for you), practice them, and open your mind to the vast options for responding mindfully, constructively, and truthfully. The more integrated the words become, the less you'll have to think. Truth will come out of your mouth with ease (and maybe even speed). Eventually you'll also find that sweet spot of healthy assertiveness, not too passive and not too aggressive.

Checking in with What You Really Want

As you start to flex your new boundary muscles, pause to take stock of what you truly desire, especially if you're prone to auto-accommodating and over-functioning. It can be helpful to buy yourself more time to assess the situation and figure out specifically what you want. For example, if someone asks you to agree to something that you're unsure of, but an immediate response feels too threatening, you can take a walk around the block or a five-minute bathroom break. That may be all the time you need to get clear on how you feel and how you're going to respond.

Here are a few ways to buy yourself some time:

- "I need a minute to regroup. Can we pick this up in a half hour?"
- "Can we chat about this later today, after I've had more time to think about it?"

Once you've reflected, you can serve up a clear, charge-free *no*, depending on the context.

- To a friend who wants you to go to a dinner that sounds shoot-me-now painful: "I'm going to say no to dinner, but I'd love to catch up another time."
- To the colleague who wants you to help with a project that is beyond the scope of your specialty, interest, or duty: "I can't, unfortunately. But once I finish up my current deadline, I'll circle back to see if there's a way I can support you."
- To the person hitting on you on the street: "Don't mind if I don't!"

Communicating When a Line Has Been Crossed

The number one challenge I see with my clients and students is uncertainty about how to tell someone that they have crossed a line. Often, if you can open up a conversation, the rest will flow. Quickly alerting the other person to your feelings, concerns, or objections can stop an easily corrected misstep or misunderstanding from turning into something more. Here are some basic conversation starters that will help you get the ball rolling:

- "I thought you should know . . ."

- "I wanted to bring something to your attention. The other day, I felt uncomfortable when . . ."

- "I need to share my experience of what went down, because I'd like you to understand how I feel and where I am coming from . . ."

- "I want you to be aware of my feelings about what happened . . ."

One of my go-to formulas for expressing a boundary violation in a charged situation is the four-part Nonviolent Communication Process we went over in chapter 7. Here's a quick review (return to page 155 for more):

"When I see that _____" (observation)

"I feel _____" (feeling)

"because my need for _____ is not met." (need)

"Would you be willing to _____?" (request)

This process is so effective because you're not calling names or making judgments. You are helping the other party understand how you feel and communicating the specific action that will alleviate your upset.

TRUE TALK *Especially in the beginning, give yourself permission to set boundaries messily, badly, or while sweating profusely. What matters most is that you do it.*

Stopping Triangulation

Triangulation is a toxic form of communication in which two people are in conflict and one enlists a third party who gets involved even though the issue doesn't directly impact them. For example, your sister borrowed your white dress shirt and returned it with a stain. She thinks you're making a big deal out of nothing. Instead of taking responsibility and offering to replace your shirt, she complains to your mother, who makes it her job to talk to you about how petty you are being. Your sister didn't have the guts to call you petty to your face, but she secretly hoped your mother would. Crazy-making, right?

Triangulation is extremely common. It happens in the workplace, with friends, and in families. Gossip and shit talking are forms of triangulation. But just because it's familiar doesn't mean it's good for anyone involved, including you.

All you need to do is opt out of being the third wheel in a toxic communication triangle. It can be as simple as saying:

- "Hey, Mom, thanks for your concern. I will hash this out with Betty directly."

With pals who like gossip, you can say:

- "Please tell me we have better things to yak about than Betty and her boy drama. What's going on with you lately?"
- "I would so much rather hear about your new job."

If you have a relative who comes to announce that your mother is "worried" about you, you can kindly nip it in the bud:

- "Thanks for your concern. I'll take it from here, Aunt Betty."

No one has the power to make you behave outside of your own integrity, even if you have in the past. Another person's bad, unconscious, or straight-up unhealthy behavior does not need to dictate yours.

Stopping the Auto Advice-Giver

If you want to share news or a personal dilemma with a pal, relative, or colleague who is often quick to give you their unsolicited opinion, you can set them up for success by starting with a qualifier, such as:

- "I have a situation I want to share with you. Can you just listen with compassion, please?"
- "I want to share what is going on for me and ask that you simply listen without offering advice or criticism. I'd really appreciate that."

If you don't preface the conversation with your desire, either because you forgot or it feels too confronting, you can halt any auto-advice (cuz you know it's coming) with:

- "At the moment, I'm not looking for feedback. I would love it if you could just lend a compassionate ear."

In relationships, especially romantic ones, where the other party has a well-established fixer role, you may want to offer more context about what you're striving for:

- "I love that you are always game to help me out. What I'd appreciate right now is for you to listen and have faith that I'll come to the answer on my own."

Deflecting Nosy Questions

Often, clients and students believe that they owe other people explanations and answers, even on minutiae. In reality, you're under no obligation to respond to nosy questions, even if they are not overtly offensive. You don't owe anyone your personal information, especially not to satisfy their curiosity.

Here are a few ways to sidestep nosy questions:

- To a love interest who asks how much money you make: "Trust me, not even close to what I'm worth."

- To a relative who asks about your love life: "I'd rather not discuss that right now. When I have news I want to share, I'll let you know."

- To a colleague who asks what you plan to do with your day off: "That's why they call it a personal day, Bob!" or "Wouldn't you like to know?" (wink)

If the person persists, repeat your stock answer. Depending on the relationship and level of aggression, you can add, "That's all I have to say on the matter."

Turning the Spotlight Away from You

If you have ever been put on the spot by a rude, invasive, or otherwise inappropriate or aggressive question or comment, you know what it's like to freeze, speechless. (And yes, this "freeze" refers to part of the fight-flight-freeze dynamic we covered in chapter 3.) Later, you may be hard on yourself, wishing you'd had the guts to say something. But when the freeze is active, courage is not the problem. Your body is simply trying to protect itself in response to a perceived threat.

Power dynamic expert Kasia Urbaniak, creator of the Verbal Self-Defense Dojo, teaches her students a strategy called "turning the spotlight" to get out of freeze and shift the power dynamics in any uncomfortable situation. The way it works is simple. Instead of answering questions that make you uncomfortable, respond with a question. You can ask a question about *their* question ("How is that relevant to you?"), or you can deflect by asking a question about something totally different ("Where did you get that cool shirt?").

Turning the spotlight works because it takes you off of center stage. When you deflect, you turn the tables. Urbaniak gives this as one of her hypothetical examples: If a male colleague asks why you don't have children, you can respond with a playful, "Why? Are you looking for a mommy?"

This example is sassy. The beauty of this approach is that you can respond in absolutely *any* way that feels right to you. Your question can be funny, flip, sassy, serious, or casual—it's your call. What matters is that you take back control by putting the other person and their bullshit behavior in the spotlight and deflecting the rude or inappropriate question.

If anyone asks you something too personal, you can turn the spotlight by saying:

- "Why do you ask?"

- "Why would you want to know that?"

- "Why would you ask me that?"

Whether you change the subject entirely or put the invasive inquirer on the spot, you have just succeeded in not answering a question that feels inappropriate. Woo-hoo!

Handling Covert Judgment

Veiled criticism can be worded in a way that *sounds* helpful or caring, but if your body wisdom starts to pipe up, you know that judgment is crossing a line.

When a friend, family member, or coworker makes a rude-as-shit comment and then says, "I'm just being honest," you may feel inclined to accept their words, even though they make you feel bad. I say, don't.

Real talk: someone who gives you genuinely constructive criticism is actually rooting for you. They care about you and are initiating a hard conversation to clue you in to something important. If you respect this person and know them to be genuine, you will likely be open to their feedback. Comments about how you wore the wrong dress or how bad your hair looks? Not constructive.

The next time someone tells you how unflattering your jeans are or reminds you of your less-than-stellar track record in love, you can say:

- "I don't recall asking you."
- "What you call honesty I call you giving me your unsolicited opinion and criticism. Please don't."

If you are in a relationship with someone who hides behind the "just being honest" shield, don't put yourself in the line of fire. For example, if your super negative friend says, "You got your hair cut," do not open the door for her to give you a wham-bam insult, by asking, "Do you like it?" You can simply say, "Yes, I did." Do not allow anyone to use their "truth" as a big stick to beat you with. When it comes to your life, your truth is the one that matters most.

It is not uncommon for religion to be used as a tool for covert judgment. I had a client who left a religious group but would still run into existing members in public. They would invariably say, "We're all praying for you." The subtext was *You are living a wrong life. We hope you get back on the righteous track soon.* She couldn't just ignore them but was unsure how to respond. We came up with a few ways for her to deflect:

- "Thank you. I'm praying for all of you, too."
- "We could *all* use some of those, thanks!"

Another effective response to someone criticizing you or acting otherwise out of bounds is to put your hand up like a stop sign.

A line has been crossed; you don't have to stand for it. A simple hand up will make your point.

Harnessing the Power of Body Language

Our body language is how we communicate through our physical behaviors, gestures, facial expressions, and more. This process can be conscious or unconscious, intentional or instinctual.

Whether you realize it or not, your body language is always broadcasting your intention and availability, long before any words have been spoken. It can strengthen or undermine your boundaries. To be most effective, your body language needs to be aligned with your desired outcome.

> **TRUE TALK** *You have trained the people in your life to treat you a certain way, and now you're retraining them based on your increased self-knowledge. Tell and show them with your words, body language, and behavior.*

For example, let's say your coworker, chatty Cathy, likes to fill you in on every detail of her dating life as she drinks her coffee in the morning, but you're not into her unsolicited stories. You could show a lack of interest by looking down, turning your body toward your computer screen, or glancing at your watch. If she still doesn't get it, then you may choose to be more direct and say, "Mornings are my most productive time, so I really need to get back to it."

Body language is also important when you run into anyone you have zero desire to engage with, like an ex, a former friend, or a nosy parent from your kid's school. Remember that your body language is *key* in this scenario. You can smile and nod in acknowledgment, but *keep walking.* You might say, "Hey there!" or "Nice to see you. Gotta run!" But the important thing is to keep on moving because nothing says "I'm not stopping to chat" like *not stopping to chat.*

Scripts for Assorted Boundary Challenges

The following are the most common boundary challenges I hear from clients and students, as well as possible scripts to address them. (You can find additional scripts in the Boundary Boss Bonus Bundle online at BoundaryBossBook.com/bonus.) As always, if a scenario doesn't fit your life or situation exactly, you can still use these suggestions as models for your own tailored responses.

Offensive Comments and Behavior

- "Racist comments are not okay with me. Stop or I'll leave."
- "Your comments/touch/words are making me uncomfortable. Please stop, or I'm going to have to leave."

Challenges to Your Deal-Breakers

- "My feelings/preferences/deal-breakers are not up for debate or discussion."

Money Matters

- "Betty, when can I expect payment for your half of our hotel bill?"
- "I'm sorry I can't help you. I have a standing policy to not lend money to friends or family."

Problem-Solving

- "I'm upset with your behavior, and because I value our relationship, I need to let you know how I feel. I hope we can come up with a satisfying solution together."

De-Escalating Conflict

- "Can I make a simple request that we circle back to this conversation after we both have had a chance to cool off?"

Saying No

- "I have other priorities, but I am sending good vibes for you to figure this one out."
- "As you know, it's my busy season at work. So, unfortunately, I won't be able to help you out with the event."
- "No, I'm sorry; I definitely can't."

Interruptions

- "Can I please finish that story? Once I finish, I'm all ears for your story about Bob."
- "When you interrupt me, it makes me feel like you're not really listening. I would like to request that you stop."

Passive-Aggression Disguised as Teasing

- "That wasn't funny to me, and I don't appreciate it."
- "Hey, you might be joking, and I am still telling you that I don't like it and want you to stop."

Someone Who Negates Your Feelings

- "I'm sharing with you how I feel, not asking for your opinion."
- "I'm telling you about *my* experience. You don't know more about my feelings than I do."

Someone Who Tries to Blame You

- "Hey, Bob, I'm not taking that on. Your choices are your own, and if you acted out of guilt or obligation, that's your business."

Chatty Hair Stylists, Massage Therapists, or Service Providers

- "I am really looking forward to some quiet time. Please don't be offended if I close my eyes."
- "I wanted to let you know in advance that I prefer a quiet massage."

Standing Up for Your Preferences

- "I know you love to plan, but I would like us to decide together when we make plans about where and when to meet."
- "I've noticed that when I am talking, you tend to get on your phone. Can I ask you to put it away and be here with me, please?"
- "That plan really doesn't work for me. Here's what I would love [insert your desired plan]. Do you have thoughts on how we can meet in the middle?"

Unhealthy Friendships (That Need to Change or to End)

- "I'm sorry; I can't make lunch/dinner/yoga." (And keep being unavailable.)
- "We seem to argue more than we get along. It's just too hard. I think we should go our separate ways."

If they argue or try to talk you out of it, you can affirm your boundary with:

- "No, this is definitely not working for me. I wish you well."
- "This friendship is not healthy for me. I wish you all the best. Please don't contact me anymore."

Bringing Up Past Grievances

For some reason, many of us believe there is a statute of limitations when it comes to addressing past grievances. I say, not true. It is never too late to attempt to be seen and heard or to honor your experiences.

- "You know, I've been thinking about an interaction we had last month/last year/in the summer of '78, and I'd like to share my thoughts and feelings about that . . ."
- "I was reflecting on something that happened last week, and it would be meaningful for me to share with you that . . ."
- "Look, I wish I had said something when this happened, but it's bothering me now, so I want to bring it to your attention . . ."

Remember, it's best to keep things simple and straightforward.

Owning Your Truth

Bottom line: the ability to set healthy boundaries in any situation is about harnessing the power of your own truth. Speaking up is extremely important and so is communicating genuine confidence in your body language. Depending on the situation, your strongest and most effective power move might be a direct look that says: *I see you, Bob. Not today, and not ever with your BS.*

As you start to get more boundary literate, you may tackle more difficult boundary scenarios, moving from practicing on lower-priority people and situations to higher-priority ones. You may start to modify your VIP list based on your discoveries. Remember: initial resistance from someone you're setting a boundary with could be a change-back maneuver and not a conscious or intentional rejection of your limits. Relying on your Proactive Boundary Plan will keep you grounded and focused on your ultimate goal: to be seen, heard, and known. The 3Qs can help you remove the historical charge from your past experiences so that you can respond in a more mindful way. The 3Rs can help you recognize, release, and respond as the Boundary Boss you know you can be.

You have trained the people in your life to treat you a certain way, and now you're teaching them a different and much better way, based on your true feelings, preferences, desires, and deal-breakers. Tell them, but also show them with your changed body language and behavior. Be bold enough to own your truth, beauty. That's what being a Boundary Boss is all about.

▶ BOUNDARY BOSS IN ACTION ◀

1. **Top of Mind.** Be aware that you are still in the In-Between. This means that as you begin to establish new boundaries, you will experience a lot of emotions. You may set a limit or make a simple request and immediately feel compelled to take it back (aka Boundary Reversal). Give yourself at least 48 hours for the anxiety to dissipate. Go to BoundaryBossBook.com/bonus for some self-soothing tips and techniques to help you through the anxiety.

2. **Go Deeper: Visualize for Next-Level Boundaries.** Now that you have the tools and the words, it's time to harness the power of visualization and create your next-level boundaries (see page 250 in the "Go Deeper" section at the back of the book).

CHAPTER 11

Life as a Boundary Boss

WOOOO-HOOOOOO!!!

Stop right now and take a moment to acknowledge just how *amazing* you are for following through and doing all of the hard work to get to this point.

Carefully assessing what's not working and swiftly pivoting into new boundary behaviors (by using the 3Rs and your Proactive Boundary Plan) becomes easier and more natural the more you do it. Taking these steps to build a life aligned with your true heart's desires is *so* worth the heavy lifting. A mini-confetti party every time you choose your own empowerment? YES, YES, YES.

Now, it's time for the next vital step: *celebrate* your efforts and wins. Every time and all the time. It is the small daily actions of prioritizing your preferences, asserting yourself, and communicating your limits and desires that create your new normal.

Becoming a Boundary Boss is not a linear path. Remember the two-steps-forward-one-step-back thing? Yeah, that's to be expected. You will succeed in some moments and fail in others, but what really matters is that you're headed in the right friggin' direction. To keep your eyes on the long-term prize, you've got to celebrate each and every mindset shift, no matter how big or small. You just respectfully declined to attend your boss's dreaded annual holiday blowout to snuggle up at home and watch movies? Amazing. You pause before saying yes because a whisper in your mind says no, thereby buying yourself time to consider your feelings and preferences first? Treat yourself to some gelato. Hell, I'd love for you to celebrate every time you recognize that you have a *choice*. *Anything* that gets you closer to your goal of conscious self-determination is cause for a moment of praise. Oh, yes. Every victory matters.

TRUE TALK *Celebrate each and every mindset shift, no matter how big or small. They are the building blocks for sustainable change.*

Practicing Self-Love

Loving ourselves is an integral part of establishing healthy boundaries. Yet for so many women I know, self-love is a nebulous concept. Many think of it as a feeling that they just don't have and will never be able to attain. Some believe that their parents' or partner's behavior toward them determines their level of lovability and dictates how much or little they can or should love themselves. By now, you are well aware of how faulty that logic is. Self-love begins and ends with you. Period.

Loving yourself authentically is less of a feeling and more of a way of life. You see it in your behaviors and choices. Drawing boundaries is one of *the* highest expressions of self-love, and that's why setting limits and establishing healthier relationships matter every damn day. If you start working out, would you expect to get the abs of your dreams in a week? Or quit as soon as you reach your goal? You would not. Learning a self-loving expression of healthy boundaries doesn't work like that, either.

Like everything else that's worthwhile, self-love is a process that requires effort. It is a series of actions that you take on your own behalf. The more you love yourself in real and tangible ways, the more you will trust yourself. Life is so much better when you know you have your own back.

BACK TO YOU:
Assessing Your Self-Care

As you know by now, good self-care is a crucial component to becoming a Boundary Boss. Use the checklist below (and feel free to add your own healthy habit if it's not listed) to get a snapshot of where your self-care is currently and whether you need to make any adjustments.

- ☐ I move my body regularly to the best of my ability.

- ☐ I eat mindfully.

- ☐ I prioritize sleep where and when I can.

- ☐ I make sure to stay hydrated throughout the day.

- ☐ I have fun regularly.

- ☐ I pay attention to my finances.

- ☐ I prioritize my comfort.

- ☐ I spend time in stillness and silence daily. (For example, practicing meditation, breathing, energy work, etc.)

Use this information to make needed changes to tune up or create a rock-solid, BB-worthy, self-care practice!

I find it telling that in my online courses and in my therapy practice, a lot of women start this work with the intention of improving their relationships, but by the time they leave, the overwhelming majority cite self-love and personal freedom as their most cherished outcomes. The two fit like a hand in a glove. Personal freedom is not possible without a foundation of self-love.

This is your life, and you come first. It is similar to the airline directive to secure your oxygen mask first, for obvious reasons. Apply that idea to everything you do. Starting from the moment you wake up in the morning, think of ways you can bring more peace, ease, and joy to your day. As a firm believer in meditation, I start my day by meditating. Sitting in stillness and silence is a fantastic act of self-love that you can practice regularly, preferably daily. Mindfulness helps to create space for more awareness.

In addition to meditation, I am also a firm believer in comfort as a core piece of self-love. Comfort is the small, feel-good touches that can make an impact on how you feel, moment to moment. I have seen, time and time again, the joy that results from something as simple as picking up fresh-cut flowers, having comfy blankets around, or stocking your cabinets with your favorite tea or salted popcorn (or whatever it is for you). Prioritizing sensual pleasures can be an effective way of staying grounded in your body, since these tiny touches invite you to be present, too. When you are truly in the moment, it's easier to breathe, to feel good, and to make the best decisions you possibly can, based on your true feelings, desires, and experiences (not on the crap in your basement). With these simple acts of self-care, you are being self-loving, not selfish.

You don't have to be rich to pay attention to the details of your life. The biggest "cost" is your own consideration, and that's a price you want to be paying. Treating yourself with the same kindness and consideration as you do others is a powerful way to support your pivot into Boundary Boss status.

Getting More Aligned

The more you head down the path of celebration and self-love, the more you may also begin to revisit old dreams or pleasures that have gone by the wayside. It's a natural process. Self-abandonment is *the* definition of Boundary Disaster-dom, and so you may have spent years drifting away from the interests that make you feel truly happy inside. But that passionate, authentic piece of yourself that loved to paint or dance, for example, never dies. It just goes underground. You're not going to feel fully self-expressed or completely joyful if parts of your true self are actively being denied or concealed. Not to mention, rediscovering these parts can be profoundly fulfilling—and a ton of fun!

Rekindling long-forgotten dreams is an essential part of the Boundary Boss way, where you align your inner world with your outer world. Witnessing women reach this part of the BB journey is thrilling.

Usually, when this part of the alignment process starts, clients will casually mention the aspirations from long ago. Some like to sing. Others like to make pottery or have always dreamt of writing a novel or starting their own business. One client was big on trapeze. Whatever the particular interest, there's almost always a naysaying voice that stops these whispered wishes in their tracks and says, "What *for*? What's the point? I'll never sell out a stadium, have a gallery show, or wind up on the bestseller list. I'll look dumb. I can't." But actually, you can—and in fact, you *must*.

You are shifting your mindset to exercise more personal agency, where you can actually taste the infinite possibilities available to you. So why wouldn't you explore something that makes you light up inside? When it comes to your soul's longing, you do not need to attach any achievement to make a particular pursuit worthy. How about saying it's worthy because you like doing it? Because it makes you feel good when you're fully immersed in doing things that bring you joy?

If you can shift your perspective on your passions, you *will* change your life. You might even wind up dreaming new dreams, more daring than you ever could have imagined. In allowing your joy to inform your behavior, you give yourself the pleasure of doing more things you love. Higher vibe, more self-expression, more feel-good hormones, you being more you, and so on. What could be better?

Keepin' It Real

The amplified energy that comes from self-celebration, self-care, and self-love is immeasurable. When we are living our truth and making empowered decisions to set healthy boundaries, we are able to give genuinely, to sprinkle our fairy dust on ourselves and those in our world, instead of having our so-called generosity giving off angsty fumes. That fairy dust is pure magic, *your* pure magic.

> **TRUE TALK** *Drawing boundaries is one of the highest expressions of self-love.*

Bringing your magic to the table will not make your life perfect. It does not mean that you'll never have moments of not wanting to make the effort or stumbling into shades of a Repeating Boundary Pattern. But if you stay the course and make self-love, self-consideration, and self-care a daily discipline, your Boundary Boss foundation will not crumble. You will be able to hold on to your personal brand of magic and recalibrate without feeling like you're in a permanent setback and there's no way forward. There is always a way forward, trust me.

In my own Boundary Boss journey, I've found that those "Oh, crap!" moments of recognizing that my basement was a-calling can actually turn into deeply healing moments of connection and love. A few years back, I was at a conference with Lara, my bestie, and we were listening to a popular spiritual figure spew some seriously arrogant BS. I found myself getting so pissed off, thinking, *This woman is a judgmental asshole. Who does she think she is?* Fed up, I walked out in the middle of her talk.

Later, over lunch, Lara asked me why I left. I started getting really heated, "She was making wrong assumptions. That woman doesn't know me!" I went on until Lara leaned in gently and said, in the most compassionate voice, "Who else didn't know you, Ter?"

Oh. A lightbulb went off. *My father.*

The speaker had pressed an ancient button and awoken residual pain of my inner child. Even though I had healed my relationship with my father before he died, I still had the occasional pang of existential sadness. I share this because you may also find yourself having occasional pangs of something you missed out on during childhood, long after you've become comfortable with healthy boundaries and self-expression.

Becoming a Boundary Boss doesn't mean you'll never have another problem or childhood-driven outburst again, but it does mean that you can handle these moments with ease and grace and use them to deepen your intimacy with yourself and others. With Lara, I had a deeply bonding conversation, and by the end, I felt more fully myself. Honoring the full range of your experiences doesn't diminish your fairy dust. On the contrary. It *increases* your magic exponentially.

Enjoying the Side Benefits of Keepin' It Real

The more real you are with yourself, the more real you can be with others, too. As a Boundary Boss, you'll start to realize that your knee-jerk reactions—from giving auto-advice to your sister-in-law, to keeping the peace at your own expense, to putting everyone else's needs above your own—aren't all that helpful, loving, or necessary. When you don't make yourself the center of other people's problems by offering up quick fixes, you get to really see the person who's in front of you, in all their beautiful, messy, and human glory. This allows you to be more human, too. As you trust your innate wisdom more, you'll naturally trust others to access their innate wisdom as well.

BACK TO YOU:
Gratitude Practice

Among other things, you have been excavating and integrating painful past experiences on your Boundary Boss journey, pinpointing what went wrong so that you can heal. Equally important is developing a regular practice of recognizing all that is right in your life, right now.

Take a moment to conjure your real feelings of gratitude for the experiences, people, or places in your life. Use the list below as a guide, and customize as needed.

- The smell of fresh coffee brewing, bread baking, or newly cut grass

- The beauty of a cityscape, a hummingbird, or a sunset

- The genius of Mahler, old Motown, or the soulful sound of Ariana Grande

- The humans who have your back, cheer you on, and want you to win

- The sound of the ocean, a baby laughing, or a bird singing

- Your favorite place to spend time and relax, like your cozy bed, a forest, a beautiful park, or your Zen Den

Did anything shift? Personally, every time I think about a baby laughing, I get a hit of joy.

Remember: where your attention goes, your energy flows. When you're feeling low, use this exercise to amplify your gratitude and elevate your mood.

Establishing healthy boundaries is not only about you being seen, heard, and known, they're also about helping you feel more connected with the people in your life. Now you have the ability to see, hear, and know them, too. Relationships without this spaciousness are never going to be fully satisfying. But ones in which both parties can support and celebrate each other's truest selves? Well, these kinds of relationships are deeply intimate and pure gold.

TRUE TALK *Your level of self-love sets the bar for every other relationship in your life. Aim high.*

Becoming clearer within yourself gives you a new perspective on other people and how they express their personal magic. Models of self-care, self-love, and general Boundary Badassery are all around us, and keeping an eye out can support your ongoing growth and expansion. As you get healthier, you may start to see others' behavior through your newly cleaned lens and be impressed by things that would have annoyed you when you were stuck in disordered boundary hell. For example, your kid's kindergarten teacher who is quick to point out that parents aren't allowed inside the building after 8 a.m. might now strike you as clear and direct, instead of bitchy (since you're no longer wading through the "let's all be fake nice" swamp). An acquaintance you once thought of as cold might seem a lot more interesting now that you're not repeating the enmeshed boundary nightmares of childhood.

Even those folks you used to feel irritated by may be cast in a different light. Now that you're considering yourself first, you can appreciate a more demanding pal's "me-first" ways which seem less offensive and more Boundary Boss-ish. You can confidently suggest a more convenient meeting spot, and then actually *enjoy* her company when you're with her, instead of seething inside or bitching about her to someone else later on. Your shifting BB perspective creates a new appreciation for others who are talking true and bidding to be seen and known authentically. You get it now.

It's Never Too Late

Years ago, I was inspired by a talk by Louise Hay, bestselling author of *You Can Heal Your Life* and founder of Hay House Publishing. She began her presentation by asking, "Who here thinks they're not where they should be in life?" A lot of hands went up. Hay said, "If I can impart one idea today, it's that you are not." She went on to share her accomplishments, including the fact that she didn't write her first book, *Heal Your Body*, until she was 50, and didn't establish Hay House, a leader in self-help book publishing, until she was 58. We are never too old or too late for true fulfillment. To this day, I still remember my own internal shift from fear to hope when I heard her words touch every single person in the audience. I left there thinking, *Maybe I'm right on time*.

Wherever you are in your life, you're right on time, too.

My hope is that you own the fact that you are a unique individual and that your choices can be informed by that uniqueness. Really, you are the only you! That's true on every level. No one else has your DNA, nor ever will. If you have a sense that you're meant to be doing more in your life, right on, celebrate! Owning your authenticity will open up some pretty incredible pathways to exploring, embracing, and expressing your own greatness.

Becoming a Boundary Boss is a choice of empowerment that will transform everything. Don't leave this life with your music still inside you, as the saying goes, because that just deprives you and the world of your unique contribution. We don't have enough bandwidth to devote ourselves to keeping the status quo *and* evolving personally. By this point, I think we can all agree that keeping the status quo is pretty overrated.

I don't know about you, but I've never heard of anyone saying on their deathbed, "I really wish I'd abandoned myself and my needs more," or "I wish I had bent over backwards to please Bob, that ingrate, just one more time." No, we tend to regret the things we *didn't* do. Ask any hospice nurse, who hears hundreds if not thousands of people's last wishes. I remember hearing a story about a woman with cancer who was facing the end of her life. She had looked at herself in the mirror and thought, *I wish I hadn't been so hard on myself.* From there, all the possibilities she'd never explored flashed in front of her eyes. When you exercise your choices from a place of solid self-love, your regrets will be minimal. The key is to remember that you *always* have choices.

In practicing self-love and healthy boundaries, you are writing the script, my dear. Would you leave your untold stories never told? Or let someone else dictate your narrative? It's what *you* think is relevant, or even priceless, that matters. Your stories are only yours to tell. No one else on this planet has the privilege of walking in your shoes, of seeing this wild and wondrous world through your eyes. If you ever have moments of feeling wrong or bad for not being like freaking Betty, know you're not. I see your light. You're amazing simply for being you.

TRUE TALK *Give yourself permission to be the one who makes decisions for you.*

When we move from a place of hiding to self-celebration, we become authentically empowered. In my view, your authentic self is not set in stone. Your authentic self must be developed and curated, as you explore and uncover your innate gifts and talents. As organizational psychologist Adam Grant says, "We don't have to be tethered to one authentic self. We can try on new identities and make them our own. We don't have to be true to ourselves.

We can be true to the selves we want to become." You have choices that impact the way you honor your authentic self. From that honoring, much more of you will develop into your truest and highest self. That is how we do the most good in the world.

If even a minuscule part of you is doubting whether you can become a Boundary Boss, I am telling you, in no uncertain terms, that you *can*. Right now is your moment. You can make that pivot now.

Whatever passages you have found especially useful in this book, take the wisdom and run with it. Make them your own. If just one line sticks with you and leads to actions or thoughts that can help you acknowledge and lessen your suffering, then my purpose has been fulfilled. The tools and strategies in this book are foundational. They will be relevant at every stage as you continue to grow and evolve for the rest of your life. As you expand, different truths will resonate. You'll see the same ideas, but they'll take on an added meaning with your continuously evolving eyes.

Dream big, and have the audacity to believe that your dreams matter, just like *you* matter. Believe in your own importance. See the value within yourself, and you will be unstoppable. The ripple effect of being real and living from your heart's truest desire is more profound than you can even imagine.

Give yourself permission to do things differently, to change your mind, to say no, to fuck up sometimes, to laugh, to sing, to smile, to dare, to simply *be*. Most importantly, be the one who makes decisions for *you*.

You got this, Boundary Boss.

And I'll be right here cheering you on like a wild maniac!

▶ BOUNDARY BOSS IN ACTION ◀

1. **Top of Mind.** Each time you carry out a new-to-you Boundary Boss response or mindset shift, celebrate. Acknowledge every new move. It might seem small, but even small changes are big. In fact, it is small, consistent steps that ultimately create sustainable transformation.

2. **Go Deeper: Explore More Tools Online.** Now is the perfect time to snuggle up in your Zen Den and explore the additional tools, strategies, therapeutically designed guided meditations, energy exercises, and so many other goodies I have for you in the Boundary Boss Bonus Bundle online at BoundaryBossBook.com/bonus. I'll see you there!

GO DEEPER

THE EXERCISES IN THIS SECTION are essential for becoming a Boundary Boss. Don't skip them!

Each one helps you integrate your understanding of Boundary Boss-ness and guides you to develop the skills necessary to put your knowledge into action. You can do many of the exercises more than once to deepen your understanding and ability.

To explore additional tools and strategies or to download and print these, check out the Boundary Boss Bonus Bundle at BoundaryBossBook.com/bonus.

CHAPTER 1:
From Boundary Disaster to Boundary Master

MAKE YOUR OWN ZEN DEN

Creating your Zen Den is simple, and you get to do it in a way that suits you.

1. **Choose a spot.** You can choose a corner of a room, an entire room, or a corner of your nightstand. Anywhere that feels inviting and comfortable.

2. **Personalize it.** Decorate it with things that feel soothing
   and inspirational—for example, a string of twinkle lights,
   a candle, a bottle of essential oil, a soft blanket or a cushion,
   or your favorite healing stones or crystals. Whatever you
   find nourishing and uplifting is 100 percent perfect.

This is your sacred space. Once you've set it up, return often to
reflect, journal, do breathing exercises, meditate, complete your BB
integration exercises, or even just to recharge for a few moments.
Can you feel that soul-exhale already?

GET YOUR MEDITATION ON

A dedicated meditation practice creates more space in you and in
your life. In fact, it can add two to three seconds of response time to
all your interactions. This essential pause allows you to respond, not
react. That is powerful.

- Start easy. At first aim to sit for five minutes. Set a timer.

- Sit down, light a candle, and take a long, slow, deep breath.

- Use a very simple Sanskrit mantra, with universal value:
  so hum, which means "I am that." Silently repeat *so* ("I
  am") on the inhalation, and then *hum* ("that") on the
  exhalation.

- Do this meditation every day, first thing if possible. Pay
  attention to what changes when you add a few minutes of
  stillness and silence to your daily routine. And once you're
  comfortable, try adding a minute a week until you reach
  twenty minutes.

To get free guided meditations, additional mindfulness tools,
and supplemental strategies, go to BoundaryBossBook.com/bonus.

CHAPTER 2:
Boundary Basics

WHAT'S OKAY/NOT OKAY

Get centered in your Zen Den, BB-in-training. Break out your journal and get ready to uncover what does and does not work for you (what's okay/not okay). The more you acknowledge what you do and don't like, the easier it will be to identify what boundaries you want in all areas of your life.

Use the questions below as a guide to write out an unedited list. You can complete it in more than one sitting, too, making notes on the fly as circumstances or situations come up. You may also find that the Okay List grows after you dive deep into the Not-Okay List. Aim to create one master list of what is currently okay/not okay in every area of your life, including your relationships.

Home. How do you prefer your surroundings to be? Think of noise level, lighting, vibe, textures, cleanliness, etc.

Work. Do you like what you are doing? Think of how you interact with coworkers, as well as the physical environment, working conditions, corporate culture, etc.

Finances. When it comes to finances, what is okay/not okay regarding your spending, saving, sharing a budget with a partner, or splitting expenses with others? Is it okay if you have a small amount of savings, or do you need to have a lot in the bank to feel okay?

Love and Dating. Do you prefer to be in a relationship or to date casually? What is your favored form of communication: text, phone, video call? How do you like to problem-solve?

How much time together or apart works for you in a relationship? What, where, when, and with whom is sex okay?

Body. Is your physical health and wellness good where it is right now? Do you have daily or weekly habits that are non-negotiable (yoga, meditation, etc.)?

Personal Space. How much do you require? Do you prefer a handshake or a hug? Do you like to be touched or not? How does it differ with close friends or a lover versus strangers and acquaintances?

Beliefs and Opinions. Are you okay when other people's beliefs and opinions differ from yours? Can you listen with an open mind, or do you become judgmental? Can you stand behind your own beliefs or opinions if someone else disapproves? Is it okay to have a spirited debate or not?

Your Stuff. Is it okay for others to borrow your possessions, eat food off of your plate, or borrow money?

Communication. Do you like a lot of communication with friends, family, and partners, or not? Do you prefer to dive deep or keep it light? Is it okay if people interrupt while you're talking?

Social. Do you prefer going out or staying in? Are group activities okay, or do you prefer more one-on-one time? Are live music, parades, parties, bars, crowds okay or not okay?

Relationships. List anything that is currently happening in any of your relationships that is not okay.

Your list will transform as your BB journey progresses. Remember: only you know what is okay and not okay for you. The more you honor your list, the more empowered and satisfied you will feel.

CHAPTER 3:
The Codependency Connection

EMOTIONAL LABOR ASSESSMENT

Use the checklist below to identify any relationships that have an unequal balance of emotional labor and where you might be taking on more than is necessary.

Emotional Labor Checklist

- ☐ I often feel like I'm doing everything for everyone.
- ☐ I wish that the people in my life acknowledged my efforts more.
- ☐ I feel overwhelmed and resentful at times.
- ☐ I often act as the go-between for the people in my life.
- ☐ If I wasn't here, nothing would get done.
- ☐ I feel responsible for fixing other people's problems and issues.
- ☐ My partner/friend/parent/boss often underestimates the time and energy required to accomplish tasks.
- ☐ I am the problem-solving point person personally or professionally.
- ☐ There are times I leave a social interaction feeling exhausted and depleted.
- ☐ I identify as a high-functioning codependent.
- ☐ I often think that if I want it done right, it is easier to do it myself.
- ☐ At times I feel inexplicably exhausted.

The more boxes you've checked, the more emotional labor you are doing.

Questions to Consider

→ Where are you volunteering to do or just *doing* more emotional labor than you need to be?

→ Where in your life are you the point person on all things?

→ Where is your partner/sibling/coworker the point person?

Make a list of the tasks, emotional and physical, that you are currently taking responsibility for, and then look to see where you can delegate, initiate conversations, and step back from over-functioning. Creating more equity in your relationships will reduce your resentment and increase your energy.

CHAPTER 4:
Corrupted Boundary Data

UNPACKING YOUR BOUNDARY BLUEPRINT

This exercise is foundational to your Boundary Boss journey. In fact, you began it in the Back to You check-in exercise on page 76 in chapter 4. But that was just a snapshot. Now, it's time to go deeper.

During your childhood, your family of origin had specific rules of engagement that informed the way members related to each other and the outside world. These rules set the stage for how well or poorly you create boundaries in your personal and professional relationships today.

Get centered in your Zen Den and read the following questions. Then, give yourself time and space to reflect, remember, and journal more on the questions you answered yes to. You may want to do this exercise over several sessions to allow your responses and insights to unfold.

→ Did you grow up in a home with abuse, addiction, strict rules, or neglect?

→ Did your parents, caregivers, or people who raised you have poor problem-solving skills? Did they respond to conflict with hostility, silence, or with verbal or physical violence?

→ Did you lack physical and material privacy? (Could you close your bedroom door? Were your things sacred, or could others take or use them? With or without your permission?)

→ Did everyone know what everyone else was doing? Were family members overly involved in each other's business and relationships?

→ Were there one or more family members who controlled others?

→ Were you punished for saying no or for not going along with the group?

→ Did your family believe there was a "right" way to do things, with little tolerance for new ideas or suggestions?

→ Were you discouraged from sharing your thoughts and feelings if they differed from the group?

→ Were you praised or rewarded for being a "good girl"? Including being compliant, agreeable, polite, and nice?

→ Were you given unasked for advice or criticism regularly?

→ Were your emotional and/or physical needs neglected?

By reflecting more deeply on your *yes* answers, you will illuminate the way your family related to each other and the outside world. Creating a detailed snapshot of your Boundary Blueprint, which will guide you on the rest of your BB journey.

CHAPTER 5:
Digging Deeper: Now Is Not Then

THE RESENTMENT INVENTORY

You alone can free yourself from the toxic prison of resentments, new or old. Becoming aware of your resentments is the first step in letting them go. The quick self-assessment tool below helps you understand how you feel and what you need. Read the questions and make a list of your answers. Then, you can decide if you need to take any action.

→ Is there anything you're feeling resentful about right now?

→ Where do you feel upset, hurt, unheard, or unseen?

→ Are there past experiences around which you still harbor resentment?

If you carry old resentments, you may want to journal about them, write a letter you never send, or, if appropriate, have a direct conversation to express your feelings. Honoring your upset is the Boundary Boss way to talk true and be seen. This exercise is for your liberation only, not to forgive or condone anyone else's behavior.

CHAPTER 6:
The 3Rs: Recognize-Release-Respond

KNOW YOUR PREFERENCES,
DESIRES, AND DEAL-BREAKERS

Now is a perfect time in your BB journey to make some fine distinctions between your preferences, desires, and deal-breakers.

Go back to the Okay/Not Okay list you created above (for chapter 2's "Go Deeper," page 239). Categorize the items in your master list according to how intensely you feel about them. Is something a preference (nice to have), a deal-breaker (cannot live without), or a desire (somewhere in between)?

Remember, you are the foremost authority on your needs. You don't need anyone's permission to feel the way you do. Reviewing your Okay/Not Okay list with an eye to your preferences, desires, and deal-breakers clarifies where you have room to compromise (a preference) and where you can't and shouldn't (deal-breakers).

NOT YOUR MAMA'S AFFIRMATIONS

An affirmation is a personal statement that can impact self-esteem, stress levels, and behaviors. What you may not realize is that negative self-talk is also affirming. But it affirms things you don't want, such as disordered boundaries.

Instead, consciously choose positive affirmations that boost self-esteem, reduce stress, and retrain your unconscious mind (which matters because your unconscious mind informs your behavior). This will help you stay focused on what you want instead of on what you fear or what you've been conditioned to expect.

Start by developing a few positive affirmation statements to repeat about yourself, your life, or the world. Then, repeat them throughout the day. To create your affirmations:

- Write in the first person (use "I").

- Use the present tense.

- Use only positive statements. Express what will be true, not what won't. For example, instead of saying, "I am no longer exhausted daily" which affirms the negative, turn it around and say, "Every day I feel more and more energized!"

- Keep it short.

- Make it emotionally meaningful to you; it needs to feel right.

- As you speak the affirmation, feel the feelings associated with it being true.

Examples to get you started:

- I love myself unconditionally.

- I express my preferences, desires, and limits with ease and grace.

- I treat myself with the same kindness and consideration I give others.

- I prioritize my pleasure daily.

- It is easy to be calm and relaxed.

When you notice negative self-talk or fear-based statements running through your mind, gently bring yourself back to your positive affirmation and *feel the feelings* associated with it. Be mindful of the fact that words have wings and creative power. They can take flight and set things in motion. Speak about yourself, your life, and your potential the way you want it to be.

You may also use more generalized affirmation statements in your everyday life. For example:

- Everything flows with ease and grace.

- I always have more than enough time.

- I am divinely guided and protected.

- I am abundant.

- All my needs are met with ease.

- I am loved.
- I am worthy.
- I am grateful for all of my blessings.

Mindfully using positive affirmations raises the energetic vibration you send out into the universe, which positively impacts the experiences you attract. This is one way to harness the mind-blowing power of your intention to create a fulfilling Boundary Boss life.

CHAPTER 7:
From Reactive to Proactive Boundaries

COMMUNICATION INTEGRITY

Many of us learned that telling little white lies to avoid conflict was harmless. For a Boundary Boss, this is not accurate, especially in high-priority relationships. Half-truths, omitting information, or tolerating the same from others to keep the peace undermines your personal power and healthy boundaries.

To assess your current communication integrity, put a check next to the behaviors that resonate with you:

- ☐ I say things I don't mean to avoid discomfort, such as accepting an invitation to an event I have no intention of attending.

- ☐ I sometimes use white lies to avoid conflict. For example, I might dodge a call from a demanding pal or say I'm eating dinner when I'm not.

- ☐ I tend to flatter others to manipulate a situation.

- ☐ I break promises to myself and others.

- ☐ I complain about pals behind their back but rarely communicate my displeasure directly.

◻ I usually remain silent instead of naming my discomfort when someone gossips, tells an offensive joke, or engages in hate speech in my presence.

◻ Even when I know that someone is being dishonest or is not keeping their word, I rarely confront them.

◻ I often make excuses about others' bad behavior instead of calling it out.

Your checked answers identify where your communication lacks integrity. Now, choose three or four of your answers. Journal about where each lack of integrity happens, when it happens, with whom, and how you feel after the interaction.

What did you learn about your patterns? Use this knowledge to make different choices next time, so you can communicate consciously and with more integrity going forward, like the Boundary Boss you were born to be!

CHAPTER 8:
Things Are Getting Real

MOURN THE DREAM

The journey to become a Boundary Boss often spotlights painful or disappointing childhood experiences. To properly honor and release them requires us to accept the way it really was and mourn the way we wished it had been. Honestly grieving your childhood disappointments without blame or judgment will free you to create more satisfaction and joy in your life now.

Do the three steps below:

1. Identify childhood disappointment(s) that you need to honor.

2. Journal about what actually happened and the way you wished it had been. Be specific about your feelings and have compassion for yourself and your pain. You may want to share what you've written with a compassionate pal or a professional to be witnessed.

3. Now, tear out that page in your journal and light it on fire in your sink, your garden, or anywhere that is safe for open flames. Ritualistic burning can be a powerful way to release the energetic hold of past disappointments. (If you can't burn it safely, you can rip it up instead.)

CHAPTER 9:
Boundary Destroyers

BOUNDARY DESTROYER HIT LIST

If you are struggling with a Boundary Destroyer, it's important to understand who you're dealing with. The first step is to take an inventory of their behaviors, including manipulation tactics, previous boundary violations, and whether your connection to this person is mandatory or optional.

Intense feelings might be activated during this exercise. Be gentle with yourself and proceed as a compassionate observer.

Use the steps below to gather information about your BDs, one at a time.

1. **The WHO:** Family, friends, romantic partners, siblings, bosses, coworkers, etc.

2. **Their BEHAVIOR:** Passive-aggressive communication, gaslighting, any form of abuse, addiction issues, love-bombing, dishonesty, _____ (add your own).

3. **The IMPACT:** Fear, anxiety, resentment, exhaustion, reduced self-esteem, financial loss, _____ (add your own).

4. **The CONNECTION:** Low priority, high priority, or mandatory (such as co-parenting).

Once you identify the existing patterns at work, you are in a far better position to act strategically and successfully. To help you craft your action plans or your next right step, refer back to page 197 in chapter 9.

CHAPTER 10:
Real-World Boundaries (Scenarios & Scripts)

NEXT-LEVEL BOUNDARIES

Now that you have the tools (Proactive Boundary Plan, the 3Rs, and scripts) to set your boundary skills in action, add visualization to your tool kit to further support your life as a Boundary Boss. Visualization can help you get out of your own way by connecting you to your desired outcomes and how they feel *before* they happen. This helps make them a reality. Allow yourself and your senses to go beyond what you know to be currently true. Instead, visualize what you *desire* to be true. Be as detailed as possible when picturing and feeling the feelings of having empowered boundary conversations.

Follow this three-step process to create next-level boundaries.

1. **See It.** Visualize yourself in an important meeting, negotiation, or annual review. Avoid focusing on what you fear might happen. (For example, that you will freeze up, agree to bad terms, and feel humiliated.) Instead, focus on what

you want to happen. In your mind's eye, see yourself strong, articulate, and empowered—no matter the outcome.

2. **Say It.** Speak positively and powerfully about yourself, your desires, and your potential. (For example, instead of affirming, "I hope I don't stumble on my words," say, "I am confident that I deserve a raise. I negotiate with ease.")

3. **Sense It.** Gently close your eyes and take a deep breath. Hold the visual you created in your mind. Next, using all of your senses, conjure the feelings of actually experiencing what you envision. (For example, the room is a perfect temperature. The chairs are comfortable. You are relaxed and confident. You speak truthfully and self-assuredly. You leave feeling proud for negotiating for your worth.)

You can apply visualization to any situation. When done consistently, it profoundly and positively impacts your ability to implement your new boundary skills every single day. Spend five minutes each morning doing this exercise to harness the incredible power of your intention.

ACKNOWLEDGMENTS

WRITING THIS BOOK TOOK A righteous village. I am deeply grateful for this incredible support.

First and foremost, to my one and only, Victor Juhasz, for his endless patience and artistic input. And for doing literally *everything* for the last year, including but not limited to shopping, cooking, laundry, pep-talking, and providing comic relief. He did it all with the same sexy good humor, generosity, and devotion he has consistently gifted me for the past 24 years. I love you the most.

I am grateful to our grown sons, Max, Alex, and Ben, and their beautiful families for inspiring me to strive to be the healthiest version of myself and for understanding my absence while in the writing cave. I love you all so much.

To my mom, Jan Cole, and my sisters, Tammi Rothstein, Kimberly Epstein, and Kathy Hughes, so much gratitude for teaching me the power of supportive sisterhood and the joy of a spontaneous dance party.

To my yayas and closest pals since Nixon was in office: Donna McKay, Carrie Godesky, Ilene Martire, Cathy McMorrow, Maureen Ambrose, and Denise Perrino for five decades of solidarity and allowing me to talk about boundaries incessantly for the past three years.

To my circle of support, inspiration, and friendship, I am blessed beyond measure: Lara Riggio, JoAnn Gwynn, Patty Powers, Danielle LaPorte, Kris Carr, Kate Northrup, Debbie Phillips, Amy Porterfield, Christina Rasmussen, Christine Gutierrez, Jessica Ortner, Julie Eason,

Davidji, Deb Kern, Gabby Bernstein, Richelle Fredson, Danielle Vieth, Latham Thomas, Elizabeth Dialto, Suzie Baleson, Carole Gladstone, and Taryn Rothstein.

To my beloved Team TC for generously picking up the slack over the past year. Special thanks to Tracey Charlebois for strategy magic plus unlimited patience and kindness. To my ride-or-die right hand, Joyce Juhasz, for keeping me organized and sane and for always having the last eyes on everything. To designer and friend Wayne Fick for making all the things look *good* and for designing the perfect *Boundary Boss* book cover.

To Suzanne Guillette, my trusted writing collaborator and friend, for coming to stay with us for a weekend planning session that turned into a three-month writing marathon. It wouldn't have happened without you.

To my literary agent, Stephanie Tade, who knew I was a writer long before I did and patiently waited a decade for me to catch on.

To everyone at Sounds True who worked tirelessly. Special thanks to Associate Publisher Jaime Schwalb for her guidance, patience, and kindness and for encouraging me to bring my unique lens to this material. To my developmental editor, Joelle Hann, whose insight and skills helped my words flow with greater ease and grace. And to Associate Acquisitions Editor Anastasia Pellouchoud for "finding" me and leading me home to Sounds True.

NOTES

Introduction

For those of you perpetually operating on get-it-done autopilot or afflicted by the disease-to-please,
> from Harriet B. Braiker in *The Disease to Please* (New York: McGraw-Hill, 2001), 1.

Chapter 1: From Boundary Disaster to Boundary Master

In the words of writer Richard Bach, "You teach best what you most need to learn,"
> from Richard Bach in *Illusions: The Adventures of a Reluctant Messiah* (London: Cornerstone, 2001), 60.

As Marianne Williamson once wrote, "It is not too late,"
> from Marianne Williamson in *The Age of Miracles: Embracing the New Midlife* (Australia: Hay House, 2013), 9.

Chapter 2: Boundary Basics

According to E. J. R. David . . . we commonly buy into the negative messages about who we are as women,
> from E. J. R. David in "Internalized Oppression: We Need to Stop Hating Ourselves," at psychologytoday.com (September 30, 2015), accessed July 13, 2020.

Eleven years later . . . Burke's campaign was reactivated and reapplied much more broadly during the sexual abuse investigation of Harvey Weinstein,
> from Sandra E. Garcia in "The Woman Who Created #MeToo Long Before Hashtags," at nytimes.com (October 20, 2017), accessed January 2020.

Good news: one year after the #MeToo movement tore through accepted prejudices,
> from Maya Salam in "A Record 117 Women Won Office, Reshaping America's Leadership," at nytimes.com (November 7, 2018), accessed January 2020.

In the wise words of meditation and mindfulness expert Davidji, "We transform the world by transforming ourselves,"
> from Davidji in *Sacred Powers: The Five Secrets to Awakening Transformation* (Carlsbad, CA: Hay House, 2017), 6.

Chapter 3: The Codependency Connection

As the pioneering clinical psychologist Dr. Harriet Lerner once wrote, "Our society cultivates guilt feelings in women,"
from Harriet Lerner in *The Dance of Anger: A Woman's Guide to Changing the Patterns of Intimate Relationships* (New York: Harper Collins, 1993), 7.

Author Gemma Hartley . . . defines emotional labor as "emotion management and life management combined,"
from Julie Beck in "The Concept Creep of 'Emotional Labor,'" at theatlantic .com (November 26, 2018), accessed March 2020.

My favorite success story about dropping emotional labor comes from Maddie Eisenhart,
from Julie Compton in "What Is Emotional Labor? 7 Steps to Sharing the Burden in Marriage," at nbcnews.com (November 9, 2018), accessed March 2020.

In addition to being hardwired to avoid rejection, a related survival instinct is the fight-flight-freeze (FFF) response,
from "Fight, Flight, Freeze," at anxietycanada.com, accessed April 2020.

Author and therapist Harper West has noted that in modern times, fight-flight-freeze is more common in response to emotional threats,
from Harper West in "How the Fight-or-Flight Response Affects Emotional Health," at harperwest.co (December 18, 2017), accessed Mach 2020.

Research suggests that chronic stress contributes to high blood pressure, among other conditions,
from "Understanding the Stress Response," at health.harvard.edu (March 2011), accessed March 2020.

She compared it to "cleansing the doors of perception,"
from William Blake in *The Marriage of Heaven and Hell* (1793), Google Books edition, accessed March 2020.

As civil rights activist and poet Audre Lorde once said, "When I dare to be powerful, to use my strength in the service of my vision, then it becomes less and less important whether I am afraid,"
from the University of New Mexico's Women's Studies Syllabus, Fall 2003, at unm.edu/~erbaugh/Wmst200fall03/bios/Lorde.htm, accessed April 15, 2020.

Chapter 4: Corrupted Boundary Data

As Louise Hay said, "The point of power is always in the present moment,"
from Louise L. Hay in *You Can Heal Your Life* (Carlsbad, CA: Hay House, 1984), 3.

Chapter 5: Digging Deeper: Now Is Not Then

In Don Miguel Ruiz's wildly popular book . . . based on ancient Toltec wisdom, the second agreement is, "Don't take anything personally,"
from Don Miguel Ruiz in *The Four Agreements* (California: Amber-Allen Publishing, 1997), 38.

According to psychologist Carl Rogers, caregivers or parents teach children conditions of worth,
> from John A. Johnson in "Agreeing with the Four Agreements," at psychologytoday.com (December 29, 2010), accessed April 2020.

The concept of Repeating Boundary Patterns was inspired by Freud's theory of repetition compulsion,
> from Kristi A. DeName in "Repetition Compulsion: Why Do We Repeat the Past?" at psychcentral.com/blog (July 8, 2018), accessed April 2020.

Chapter 6: The 3Rs: Recognize-Release-Respond

In fact, the brain's neural connections—estimated to be in the ballpark of a whopping 100 trillion—are formed and potentially altered every single day,
> from Melinda T. Owens and Kimberly D. Tanner in "Teaching as Brain Changing: Exploring Connections between Neuroscience and Innovative Teaching," CBE Life Sciences Education (Summer 2017), at lifescied.org, accessed March 14, 2020.

Chapter 7: From Reactive to Proactive Boundaries

It isn't part of the process; it is the process,
> from Davidji in "Change Is Breath Meditation Metta Moment," at davidji.com (November 5, 2019), accessed April 2020.

That Gus sabotaged her efforts after initially agreeing to support her is a classic change-back maneuver,
> from Harriet Lerner in "Coping With Countermoves," at psychologytoday.com (December 20, 2010), accessed April 2020.

The steps below are based on the four-part Nonviolent Communication Process developed by Marshall B. Rosenberg, PhD,
> from Marshall B. Rosenberg and Arun Gandhi in *Nonviolent Communication: A Language of Life: Create Your Life, Your Relationships, and Your World in Harmony with Your Values* (Encinitas, CA: PuddleDancer Press, 2003).

The same brain circuits that are responsible for mind wandering also help us retain our sense of self and understand what others are thinking more accurately,
> from David Rock in "New Study Shows Humans Are on Autopilot Nearly Half the Time," at psychologytoday.com (November 14, 2010), accessed March 2020.

Chapter 8: Things Are Getting Real

As you can imagine, these painful childhood experiences become ingrained and keep us in survival mode,
> from Susan Peabody in "Toxic Guilt," at thefix.com (April 27, 2018), accessed April 2020.

As energy medicine expert . . . Lara Riggio likes to say, "Upset is access,"
    from Lara Riggio in "How to Tap Out Negative Thoughts, and Focus Your Energy on What You Want Instead," at larariggio.com, accessed April 2020.

Social scientist Brené Brown . . . says that three things keep shame in the driver's seat of your life,
    from Brené Brown in "Listening to Shame," a TED Talk filmed in March 2012, at ted.com, accessed April 2020.

I love the juxtaposition that psychologist Kristin Neff, cofounder of the Center for Mindful Self-Compassion, makes: "Unlike self-criticism, which asks if you're good enough, self-compassion asks, 'What's good for you?'"
    from Madhuleena Roy Chowdhury in "Kristin Neff and Her Work on Self-Compassion," at positivepsychology.com (October 25, 2019), accessed April 2020.

Chapter 9: Boundary Destroyers

If leaving or having no contact is not an option, the Gray Rock method, essentially becoming bland and unreactive, will help you become a less interesting target,
    from Darlene Lancer in "The Price and Payoff of a Gray Rock Strategy," at psychologytoday.com (November 4, 2019), accessed April 2020.

Lindsey Ellison . . . advises treating communication with narcissists like a business transaction,
    from Lindsey Ellison in *Magic Words: How to Get What You Want from a Narcissist* (Toronto, Ont.: Hasmark Publishing, 2018).

Chapter 10: Real-World Boundaries (Scenarios & Scripts)

One of my go-to formulas for expressing a boundary violation in a charged situation is the four-part Nonviolent Communication Process,
    from Marshall B. Rosenberg's "The 4-Part Nonviolent Communication Process" (PDF), at nonviolentcommunication.com, accessed April 18, 2020.

Power dynamic expert Kasia Urbaniak . . . teaches her students a strategy called "turning the spotlight" to get out of freeze and shift the power dynamics in any uncomfortable situation,
    from kasiaurbaniak.com, accessed April 18, 2020.

Chapter 11: Life as a Boundary Boss

As organizational psychologist Adam Grant says, "We don't have to be tethered to one authentic self,"
    from Adam Grant in "Authenticity Is a Double-Edged Sword," at ted.com /podcasts/worklife, accessed April 10, 2020.

ABOUT THE AUTHOR

TERRI COLE is a New York–based licensed psychotherapist, relationship expert, and founder of Real Love Revolution, Boundary Bootcamp, and the cofounder of Crushing Codependency, female empowerment courses that reach women in over ninety countries.

Prior to her current incarnation as a love and boundaries expert, Terri was a bicoastal talent agent, negotiating endorsement contracts for supermodels and celebrities. Her eventual disenchantment with the world of entertainment led her to change her career in her thirties, when she became a psychotherapist and female empowerment expert. She has since made it her mission to teach as many women as possible to establish and maintain effective boundaries with ease and to create and sustain healthy, vibrant relationships. For the past two decades, Terri has worked with some of the world's most well-known personalities, from international pop stars, athletes, Broadway performers, and TV personalities, to thought leaders and Fortune 500 CEOs. She empowers over 450,000 people weekly through her published articles and blog posts, illuminating videos, therapeutic meditations, online courses, and her popular podcast, *The Terri Cole Show*.

Terri's approach combines the best of practical psychology and Eastern mindfulness practices. She has a gift for making complex psychological concepts accessible and actionable, so that clients and students achieve sustainable change, i.e., true transformation.

ABOUT THE AUTHOR

She has been featured as an expert therapist and master life coach on A&E's *Monster In-Laws*, TEDx, *The Lisa Oz Show*, *Real Housewives*, and she had a weekly radio show on Hay House Radio. Terri has been a contributor to *HuffPost*, Positively Positive, The Daily Love, Well+Good; has been featured in *Woman's Day*, *Psychology Today*, *The Boston Globe*, *Italian Elle*, *Forbes*, *Origin*, CNN, *Vogue*, *Self*; and was honored to grace the cover of *Inspired Coach* magazine.

Learn more about her work at terricole.com.

ABOUT SOUNDS TRUE

SOUNDS TRUE is a multimedia publisher whose mission is to inspire and support personal transformation and spiritual awakening. Founded in 1985 and located in Boulder, Colorado, we work with many of the leading spiritual teachers, thinkers, healers, and visionary artists of our time. We strive with every title to preserve the essential "living wisdom" of the author or artist. It is our goal to create products that not only provide information to a reader or listener but also embody the quality of a wisdom transmission.

For those seeking genuine transformation, Sounds True is your trusted partner. At SoundsTrue.com you will find a wealth of free resources to support your journey, including exclusive weekly audio interviews, free downloads, interactive learning tools, and other special savings on all our titles.

To learn more, please visit SoundsTrue.com/freegifts or call us toll-free at 800.333.9185.